商务英语专业中高职一体化系列教材

总主编 李德荣

Telephone Skills

电话交流技能

主编／陈文珊

上海商贸职业教育集团 组织编写

图书在版编目(CIP)数据

电话交流技能＝Telephone Skills：英汉对照／陈文珊主编．—上海：立信会计出版社，2012.9
商务英语专业中高职一体化系列教材
ISBN 978-7-5429-3622-6

Ⅰ.①电… Ⅱ.①陈… Ⅲ.①英语—口语—高等职业教育—教材 Ⅳ.①H319.9

中国版本图书馆 CIP 数据核字(2012)第 184080 号

策划编辑　徐雪芬　张　寻
责任编辑　余　榕　周　瑜
封面设计　周崇文

Telephone Skills——电话交流技能

出版发行	立信会计出版社		
地　　址	上海市中山西路 2230 号	邮政编码	200235
电　　话	(021)64411389	传　　真	(021)64411325
网　　址	www.lixinaph.com	电子邮箱	lxaph@sh163.net
网上书店	www.shlx.net	电　　话	(021)64411071
经　　销	各地新华书店		

印　　刷	常熟市梅李印刷有限公司	
开　　本	787 毫米×1092 毫米	1/16
印　　张	13	
字　　数	329 千字	
版　　次	2012 年 9 月第 1 版	
印　　次	2012 年 9 月第 1 次	
印　　数	1—3100	
书　　号	ISBN 978-7-5429-3622-6/H	
定　　价	28.00 元	

Perface
总 序

中国的企业正在向与国际接轨的现代企业转型。这一转型就宏观层面而言，是一种文化的转型。其成功与否，取决于能否借鉴世界上(尤其是发达国家和地区)已被证明为成功的企业管理文化。企业管理文化博大精深，至关重要。它大可涉及国计民生、社会安定、企业责任、管理风格，小可涉及计划安排、日常管理、服务态度、待人接物。这一文化是整个社会文化的一个重要组成部分，且直接影响人民生活。令人遗憾的是，对这一文化至今尚缺少应有的关注和倡导。

上海商贸职业教育集团根据国家经济发展战略和教育部构建现代职业教育体系的要求，从 2009 年起致力于各级各类职业教育协调发展的研究和中高职教育有效衔接的实践，完成了中高职教育定位正确、专业培养目标与职业岗位培养方向对接、学历证书与人力资源和社会保障局职业资格证书融通的《会计》、《市场营销/连锁经营管理》、《金融事务》、《国际商务》、《现代物流》、《应用艺术设计》、《酒店管理》和《商务英语》8 个中高职教育专业教学方案。其中《商务英语》是基于国际化视野、有机融入企业文化、所有课程进一步突出能力标准的全新开发的专业教学方案。

《商务英语》专业教学方案致力于引进新的国际教育教学理念，从理论到操作层面对旧的课程设置和教学内容进行改革，使之既与国际接轨，同时又适合中国国情。该教学方案大力引进国外课程，解决英语学习和专业学习的矛盾，意在终结英语学习和专业学习"两张皮"的历史，并探索中高职教育如何实现有效衔接或在一体化的研究中取得积极的进展。项目论证的有关专家一致认为，新方案从实际而非概念出发，借鉴发达国家成功经验，大胆创新，为中高职商务英语专业的发展，开创了值得努力探索和实践的新道路。

该专业教学方案配套教材计划开发 12 种，按教学进程需要，我们将以下 8 门课程列入首批编写，这些课程包括《企业与社会》、《电话交流技能》、《工作场所交流技能》、《工作文件写作》、《商务谈判》、《管理学基础》、《国际贸易》和《营销学基础》。这些教材以英语为载体，介绍先进的企业管理文化，同时具有语言教材的一些特点，使之适合中国学生学习。与传统教材相比，新教材具有下列特点：

1. 专业课程体现专业特色，迈出与国际接轨的步伐

以往的专业课程没有明确的规定和规范，各校根据自身的条件和情况开设，有的侧重外贸，有的侧重营销，也有的将重点放在开设一些单证、报关等实务课程。新教材积极借鉴国外相关经验，从培养目标出发，以“能用英语从事商务活动”为教改基本思想，以英语应用能力和商务实践能力为重点，以求达到“知识型、发展型技能人才”的培养目标。把商务专业知识的学习与英语学习自然地融合在一起，让学生既学专业，又学英语，两者相辅相成，相得益彰。

2. 切实做到中高职课程衔接

以往中高职互不通气，各行其是，所开设的课程有相似，亦有重复，非常不利于专业建设。新教材对中高职课程进行了明确的界定，即使是同一门课程，对课程内容和教学方式也作了明确的区分，尤其是对“双语”、“全英语”的界定，保证了中高职课程的有效衔接。

3. 标准细化，便于操作

新教材对课程的知识和技能要求作了全新的诠释和详尽的规定，由浅入深，知行一体，经过一定的教学思想的提示，十分有利于课程的实施。在体例上，这套教材既是专业教材，又具有语言教材的特点。在介绍专业知识的同时，对专业知识的语言载体——包括词汇、句型、习惯用法、商务英语的特点等用注释、标示及各类练习等手段，让学生掌握并应用，提高英语水平。这一新的尝试，旨在努力改变以往商务英语专业存在的英语学习和专业学习“两张皮”的状况，开创一条专业学习与英语学习融合的新路。

4. 运用先进的教学理念

教材从内容到形式均为创新型教材，从教学内容到教学手段，既充分与国际接轨，同时又适合于中国学生，为国内首创。在专业知识介绍方面，内容上力求基础、实用，文字上力求简明、通俗，以适合职业教育的特点和学生现有的英语水平。

我国的职业教育与发达国家相比差距很大。这也使它具有较大的发展空间和创新空间。职业教育的发展需要更多的关注、关心和扶持。本套教材系新创，问题和不足在所难免，希望广大教师在使用中提出宝贵的修改意见，以使本套教材得到不断完善。

上海商贸职业教育集团常务副理事长

冯伟国

2012 年 8 月 12 日

Telephone Skills

Foreword
前 言

随着当今世界经济全球化进程的加快和中国经济的蓬勃发展，社会对能够从事跨文化交际和开展国际商务活动的职业人员的需求日益增加。使用电话进行跨国跨文化交流成为商务活动中不可缺少的一部分。为了满足中高职商务英语专业学生对用英语进行电话沟通交流的技能的需求，商务英语电话技能的教学也成为各中高等职业学校的重要任务。

本教材是中高等职业学校商务英语专业教学用书，由长期从事职业教育工作的教师针对中高职学生的年龄特点和学习习惯精心编写而成，同时可供有相同需求专业(如国际贸易、国际营销、涉外旅游等)的学生使用。目录中加有星号“*”的部分供中职学校使用。

本教材具有以下特点：

(1) 以《中高职衔接商务英语专业标准》和《电话英语技能》课程标准为编写依据，以就业为导向，并充分考虑中高职学生教育的年龄特点和认知水平。

(2) 采用大量的商务电话作为材料，帮助学生获取足够的感性知识，同时体现“内容教学”的特点，展示了一个真实的商务活动的面貌。教材内容具体丰富，涉及商务活动多方面的话题，具有很强的实用性，能满足中高职学生今后用英语从事商务工作的需要。

(3) 本教材的设计尤为注重中高职学生英语听说技能的培养，练习形式具有多样化，在难度上循序渐进，在帮助学生获得电话接听技能同时，提高英语综合能力。

本教材由上海市工商外国语学校陈文珊主编，参加编写的有陈文珊、陈明娟、谢永业、伍梅、付慧、徐晓慧、曹红莲、王烨、唐菲等。在编写过程中，编者参阅了大量的国内外相关资料，在此谨向这些资料的作者表示衷心的感谢。

为方便教学，本书配有录音和习题参考答案，需要的读者可访问 www.lixinaph.com 获取。

由于编者水平有限，因此在编写过程中难免会有不当和疏漏之处，恳请广大师生和读者不吝赐教，使本教材不断完善。

编　者

2012年8月

Telephone Skills

CONTENTS

目 录

Unit 1 Receiving and Responding to Calls 1

1. Opening and Closing* (Telephone Conversations 1 – 5) 3
2. Identifying Caller's Needs & Providing Information* (Telephone Conversations 6 – 10) 13
3. Connecting and Transferring Calls* (Telephone Conversations 11 – 15) 24
4. Voice Mail & Taking Telephone Messages* (Telephone Conversations 16 – 20) 35
5. Providing Information & Explanation (Telephone Conversations 21 – 25) 45
6. Delivering Messages (Telephone Conversations 26 – 30) 56
7. Dealing with Complaints (Telephone Conversations 31 – 35) 65

Unit 2 Making Calls 75

1. Completing Simple Business Tasks* (Telephone Conversations 36 – 40) 77
2. Completing More Complicated Business Tasks* (Telephone Conversations 41 – 45) 88
3. Discussing Business Issues (Telephone Conversations 46 – 50) 99
4. Establishing Business Relations (Telephone Conversations 51 – 55) 110
5. Seeking Information about Products & Services (Telephone Conversations 56 – 60) 122
6. Seeking Information about Prices & Contracts (Telephone Conversations 61 – 65) 135
7. Negotiating with Clients (Telephone Conversations 66 – 70) 145

Unit 3 The Telephone System ························ 157

1. The Telephone* ························ 159

2. Landline Telephones* ························ 164

3. Mobile Phones* ························ 169

4. Internet Telephones* ························ 173

5. Telephone Functions ························ 178

6. Domestic Telephone Systems ························ 182

7. International Telephone Systems ························ 188

8. Basic Telephone Skills and Techniques ························ 193

Unit 1

Receiving and Responding to Calls

1. Opening and Closing *

(Telephone Conversations 1 - 5)

Telephone Conversation 1

New Words and Expressions

international telephone service 国际电话服务
collect call 对方付费电话
dial *v.* 拨号
accept the charges 接受付费
connect *v.* 接通(电话)

Caller 1：International telephone service. May I help you?
Caller 2：Yes，I'd like to make a collect call to Los Angeles 712 - 2134.

Caller 1：Your name，please.
Caller 2：Mary Smith.

Caller 1：Miss Smith，and who do you wish to speak to?
Caller 2：Jim Ted.
Caller 1：Just a moment，please. (dialing)

Caller 3：Hello.
Caller 1：I have a collect call for you from Mary Smith. Will you accept the charges?

Caller 3：Of course.
Caller 1：(To Smith) I've connected your call. Go ahead，please.

Caller 2：Mr. Ted，is that you?
Caller 3：Yes，is that Mary Smith?

Exercise A：Answer the following questions.

1. Who does Miss Smith want to call?
2. What kind of call does Miss Smith want to make?
3. Who puts through the collect call?

Exercise B：Listen to the conversation and fill in the blanks.

1. ____________________. May I help you?
2. I'd like to make ____________________ to Los Angeles 712 - 2134.
3. Who do you wish to ____________ to?
4. ____________________，please.
5. I have a collect call for you from Mary Smith. Will you accept ____________?
6. I've ____________ your call. Go ahead，please.

Exercise C：Role play.

Mary White from Kennedy Company wants to make a collect call to New York 638 - 3829，Mr. Frank Lee.

Telephone Conversation 2

New Words and Expressions

director *n.* 主任；经理
human resources 人力资源
insurance *n.* 保险(公司)
in regards to 关于
available *a.* 在的，可得到的
leave a message 留口信
get in touch with 与……取得联系

Caller 1：Hello，thank you for calling Black and Sons. This is Jenny speaking. How may I help you?
Caller 2：Hello. I would like to speak to your director of human resources，Ms. Watson，Please.

Caller 1：Just a moment. I'll check to see if she is at her desk. May I tell her who is calling?

Caller 2：This is Peter Burton from Peace Insurance. I'm calling in regards to our meeting next Wednesday.

Caller 1：Thank you，Mr. Burton. Can you please hold for a moment? I'll check to see if she is available[1].

Caller 2：No problem.

Caller 1：I'm sorry. Ms. Watson is away from her desk. She has already left for lunch. Would you like to leave a message for her?

Caller 2：Yes，please have her return my call when she returns to the office[2]. It's best if she can get in touch with me before 3 p. m. today；she can reach me at my office number，635－8799[3].

Caller 1：I will make sure[4] Ms. Watson receives your message and returns your call before 3 p. m. this afternoon.

Caller 2：Thank you very much.

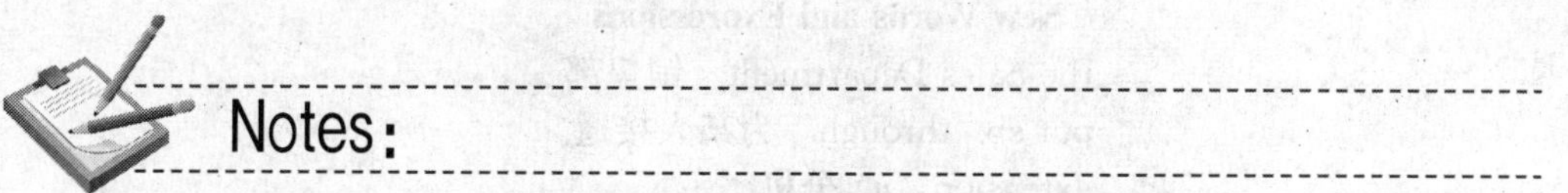

1. I'll check to see if she is available：我确认一下她是否在办公室。
2. please have her return my call when she returns to the office：她回办公室后请让她打电话给我。
3. She can reach me at my office number，635－8799：她拨打我办公室的电话 635－8799 便可找到我。
4. I will make sure ...：我一定会……

Exercise A：Answer the following questions.

1. Which company is Jenny from?
2. Who would Peter like to speak to?
3. Which company is Peter from?
4. Why isn't Ms. Watson in the office?
5. What's the message left by Peter?
6. What will Jenny make sure?

Exercise B：Listen to the conversation and fill in the blanks.

1. Hello，thank you for calling ________________.
2. I would like to speak to your director of ________________，Ms. Watson，Please.

3. I'll ________________ to see if she is at her desk.
4. Would you like to ________________ for her?
5. I'm calling ________________ our meeting next Wednesday.
6. It's best if she can ________________ me before 3 p. m. today.

Exercise C: True or false. Correct the false statements.

1. Peter is calling to speak to Ms. Watson.
2. Peter is the director of human resources.
3. Ms. Watson is away from her desk because of a meeting.
4. Peter's home number is 635 - 8799.
5. Ms. Watson will certainly receive Peter's message and return his call before 3 p. m. this afternoon.

Telephone Conversation 3

New Words and Expressions

the Sales Department 销售部
put sb. through 为某人接通
extension *n.* 分机
Ltd.(= Limited) 有限公司
engaged *a.* 占线的
equipment *n.* 设备
order *v.* 订购

Caller 1: Good afternoon, Mr. Black's office. Can I help you?
Caller 2: Good afternoon, I'd like to speak to Mr. Steven, please.

Caller 1: Mr. Steven works in the Sales Department. Hold the line, please. I'll put you through to the extension of the Sales Department.
Caller 3: Sales Department, Wang Lin speaking.

Caller 1: A caller on the line for Mr. Steven[1].
Caller 3: I'll get him.

Caller 1: Thank you. (to the caller) Through now.
Caller 2: Thank you very much. Hello, this is Mary Anderson of General Cars Ltd. I'd like to speak to Mr. Steven, please.

Caller 4：Steven speaking. Hello，Mr. Anderson. I phoned you a moment ago，but your line was engaged[2]. How is the equipment you ordered ...

Notes:

1. A caller on the line for Mr. Steven：线上有人打电话找史蒂文先生。
2. I phoned you a moment ago, but your line was engaged：我刚刚给你打电话，但电话占线。

Exercise A：Answer the following questions.

1. How many persons are there in the phone call?
2. Which company is Miss Huang from?
3. Who is calling?
4. Who is wanted on the phone?
5. Which department is Mr. Steven in?
6. What's the probable relationship between Wang Lin and Mr. Steven?

Exercise B：Listen to the conversation and fill in the blanks.

1. Good afternoon，________________. Can I help you?
2. Mr. Steven works in __________________________.
3. __________________________，Wang Lin speaking.
4. ________________ on the line for Mr. Steven.
5. This is Mary Anderson of ________________.
6. I phoned you a moment ago, but your line was ________________.

Exercise C：Read the following passage and choose the correct answer.

Today people can use the phone to talk with others almost anywhere on the earth. But when you use the phone，you don't see the person you are talking with. That may change in the near future.

Today some people are using a kind of telephone called the picture phone or vision phone. With it，two people who are talking can see each other.

Picture phones can be useful when you have something to show the person you're calling. They may have other uses in the future. One day you may be able to ring up a library and ask to see a book. Then you'll be able to read the book right over your picture phone. Or you may be able to go shopping through your picture phone. If you see something in the newspaper that you think you want to buy，you'll go to your phone and call the shop. People at the shop will show you the thing you're interested in right over the phone. You'll be able to shop all over the town and never leave your room!

1. Today people can use the phone to talk with others ________.
   A. in all the towns B. in some places in the world
   C. only in big cities D. almost anywhere on the earth
2. The word "it" in the passage means ________.
   A. the picture phone B. any phone
   C. the use D. the change
3. We can ________ through the picture phone according to the passage.
   A. write a book B. do some shopping
   C. play games D. have classes
4. Picture phones are very ________.
   A. useful B. impossible C. bad D. badly
5. Which is not true according to the passage?
   A. Today some people are using a kind of telephone called the picture phone or vision phone
   B. With the picture phone, two people can't see each other
   C. The phone is very useful
   D. Today people can use the phone to talk with others almost anywhere on the earth

Telephone Conversation 4

New Words and Expressions

run into 遇上
unexpected *a.* 出乎意料的
senior *a.* 高级的,资深的
troublemaker *n.* 捣乱者
fire *v.* 开除
intend *v.* 打算
personal *a.* 私人的
demand *v.* 要求

(*Sometimes a secretary may run into some unexpected telephone calls. The following is an example. You will see how Miss Zhang, a senior secretary, deals with the troublemakers'*[1].)

Caller 1: Mr. Hansen's office, Miss Wang speaking.
Caller 2: I want to talk to Mr. Ramon Hansen.
Caller 1: May I have your name, sir?

Caller 2：I'm Tom Smith.

Caller 1：May I tell Mr. Hansen the reason for your call，Mr. Smith?

Caller 2：He fired my cousin yesterday，and I intend to talk to him about it.

Caller 1：I'm sorry，but Mr. Hansen is very busy right now. Perhaps you would like to write him a letter about the situation. If you will mark it "Personal"，I will see that it comes to his attention[2].

Caller 2：No，I demand to talk to him.

Caller 1：I'm very sorry，Mr. Smith，but I can't help you. Good-bye.

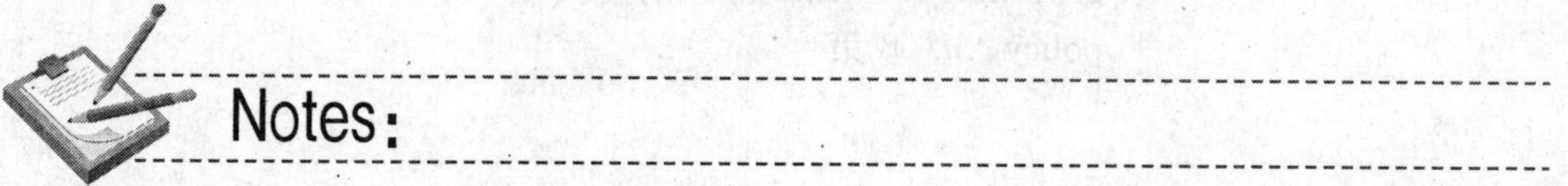

1. You will see how Miss Zhang，a senior secretary，deals with the troublemakers'：你会看到资深秘书张小姐是如何应付捣乱者的电话的。
2. If you will mark it "Personal"，I will see that it comes to his attention：如果您在信封上标明"私人信件"，我想这会引起他的注意。

Exercise A：Listen to the conversation and fill in the blanks.

1. Sometimes a secretary may run into some ________________ telephone calls.
2. May I have ____________，sir?
3. May I tell Mr. Hansen ________________________ your call，Mr. Smith?
4. Perhaps you would like to write him a letter about ________________.
5. If you will mark it "Personal"，I will see that it comes to ________________.
6. I ______________ to talk to him.

Exercise B：Listen to the conversation and fill in the form.

From	
To	
Problem(s)	
How to solve it/them?	

Exercise C：Writing.

Suppose you are Tom Smith，write a letter to Mr. Hansen to talk about the matter.

Telephone Conversation 5

New Words and Expressions

appointment *n.* 约会
president *n.* 总经理
urgent *a.* 紧急的
cancel *v.* 取消
put off 推迟
in the first place 一开始;首先
government officials 政府官员
policy *n.* 政策

Caller 1: Good afternoon. May I speak to Mr. Brown?
Caller 2: This is Brown speaking. Who's calling, please?

Caller 1: This is Tian Hua from Red Star Pen Factory.
Caller 2: Oh, Miss Tian, what's happened?

Caller 1: It's about the appointment with our president. I'm extremely sorry she can't see you at 2 o'clock this afternoon. You see, something unexpected has come up[1]. She has to attend an urgent meeting.
Caller 2: So you want to cancel the appointment. That's too bad.

Caller 1: No, not exactly. Actually we just want to put it off until supper time. After that we'll invite you to dinner.
Caller 2: Well, so much the better. Why didn't you mention it in the first place?

Caller 1: I only want to give you a surprise[2]. We have also invited government officials to be present at the dinner and you can learn more about the new policy.
Caller 2: That's wonderful. Thank you very much for what you have done for us.

Notes:

1. Something unexpected has come up: 发生了一件意外的事情。
2. give you a surprise: 给你一个惊喜。

Exercise A: Answer the following questions.

1. Who is calling to Mr. Brown?
2. Does Miss Tian want to cancel the meeting?
3. Why can't the president see Mr. Brown at 2 o'clock this afternoon?
4. When will the meeting be put off?
5. Why doesn't Miss Tian say that in the first place?
6. What's the surprise?

Exercise B: Listen to the conversation and fill in the blanks.

1. Oh, Miss Tian, ______________?
2. I'm ______________ she can't see you at two o'clock this afternoon.
3. You see, something unexpected has ______________.
4. So you want to ______________ the appointment.
5. Actually we just want to put it off until ______________.
6. We have also invited some of the government officials to be present at the dinner, so that you can ______________ something about the policies.

Exercise C: Arrange the order of the events.

A. The president from Red Star Pen Factory has a meeting with Mr. Brown.
B. They have a dinner with some of the government officials and talk about something about the policies.
C. Something unexpected has come up.
D. Tian Hua calls Mr. Brown.

Practice

I. Translate the following phrases into Chinese.

1. deal with
2. make sure
3. human resources
4. a collect call
5. put through
6. a moment ago
7. put off
8. in regards to
9. find out
10. get in touch with

II. Fill in the blank with the phrases in Exercise I.

1. I'd like to make ______________ to New York 642 - 3294.
2. I'll ______________ you ______________ ... (to the extension of the Sales Department)
3. I would like to speak to your manager of ______________, Mr. Smith, please.
4. I phoned you ______________, but your line was engaged.
5. Actually we just want to ______________ it ______________ until this afternoon.
6. I'm calling ______________ our appointment tomorrow morning.
7. You will see how the experienced secretary will ______________ the troublemakers'.

8. We have also invited some experts to be present at the lecture, so that you can ________ ______ something about the project.
9. I will ______________ Ms. Keller receives your message and returns your call before 8 p. m. tomorrow.
10. It's best if she can ______________ me before 3 p. m. today.

III. Listen to the following conversation and fill in the blanks.

1. What date would you like to make a ______________ for?
2. I only handle bookings for our ______________.
3. Could you please ______________ your last name for me?

IV. Role-play.

You are calling Miss White, vice-manager of Zhonghua Company. You want to tell her that your manager Mr. Wang can't attend the meeting to be held tomorrow morning and you want to put off the meeting to the day after tomorrow. Because Miss White has to go abroad, the meeting will be put off to next Wednesday.

2. Identifying Caller's Needs & Providing Information *

(Telephone Conversations 6 - 10)

Telephone Conversation 6

New Words and Expressions
be off sick 因生病不在
spell *v.* 拼写
surname *n.* 姓
confirm *v.* 确认
budget *n.* 预算
annual *a.* 每年的,年度的
figure *n.* 数字

Caller 1：Solomo Company.
Caller 2：Hello. May I speak to Roderick Pritchett，please?

Caller 1：I'm afraid he is off sick. Would you like to leave a message?
Caller 2：Yes，my name is Alexandra Barrett.

Caller 1：Could you spell your surname，please?
Caller 2：Sure. B-A-R-R-E-T-T.

Caller 1: And what is the message?
Caller 2: I can't fly to Sydney on 11 May. There is no place available[1]. But I can come on the 12th. Could you ask Roderick to confirm that he can see me on the 12th?

Caller 1: Sure, and anything else?
Caller 2: He needs my budget figures for the annual report[2]. I'm afraid they're not ready yet, and I'd like to check them again. Some of the figures aren't quite right. I'll email them to him this afternoon.

Caller 1: Well, does he have your number?
Caller 2: Yes, he does.

Caller 1: All right, Ms. Barrett, I'll give your message to Mr. Pritchett.
Caller 2: Thanks.

Caller 1: You're welcome. Good-bye.
Caller 2: Bye-bye.

Notes:

1. There is no place available：没有位子了。
2. annual report：年度报告。

Exercise A: Answer the following questions.

1. Why doesn't Roderick Pritchett in?
2. Why cannot Ms Barrett fly to Sydney on 11 May?
3. When will Ms Barrett fly to Sydney?
4. What does Alexandra Barrett need?
5. Why aren't the budget figures ready?
6. When will Ms Barrett send the figures to Roderick Pritchett?

Exercise B: Listen to the conversation and fill in the blanks.

1. I'm afraid he is ________ ________. Would you like to leave a message?
2. I can't fly to Sydney on 11 May. There is no place ________.
3. But I can come on the 12th. Could you ask Roderick to ________ that he can see me on the 12th?
4. He needs my ________ figures for the ________ report.
5. I'm afraid they're not ready yet, and I'd like to ________ them again.

6. Some of the figures aren't quite right. I'll ________ them to him this afternoon.

Exercise C: Making sentences by using the words and expressions of this unit.

Telephone Conversation 7

New Words and Expressions
item *n.* 物品
carton *n.* 箱
suit *n.* (一套)衣服
order number 订单号
discount *n.* (打)折扣
volume of trade 贸易量
improve *v.* 改进

Caller 1: Good morning, George's Beauty Clothing[1] Ltd, what can I do for you?
Caller 2: Good morning. This is Helen Chandra form ABC Company. I'd like to speak to Joe Panetta.

Caller 1: Yes, Joe's speaking. Can I help you?
Caller 2: Our order has arrived, but you've sent the wrong items. We ordered thirty cartons of T-shirts, fifty cartons of trousers, and two cartons of suits. You sent us thirteen cartons of T-shirt, fifteen cartons of trousers, and the wrong suits.

Caller 1: I'm terribly sorry about that. If you don't mind, could you tell us your order number? I'll check it for you.
Caller 2: DDJAT76481002.

Caller 1: Wait for a moment. Err ... could you tell me which suits you ordered?
Caller 2: Well, the code is JD 5040, but the code on the ones we received is JD 5014.

Caller 1: I am awfully sorry for the mistake made by our company. We'll send you the right order as soon as possible and we'll also give you a 10% discount[2].
Caller 2: Thanks. I hope the volume of trade between us will be even greater in the future.

Caller 1: We'll also do everything to improve our service.
Caller 2: Well, thanks for your help. Good-bye.

Caller 1：It's my pleasure[3].

Notes：

1. beauty clothing：美容服饰。
2. give you a 10% discount：给你 10%的折扣。
3. It's my pleasure：很高兴为您服务。（常用的客套话）

Exercise A：Answer the following questions.

1. Which company does Joe Panetta work for?
2. What happened when Helen received the order?
3. What is the order number?
4. Which suits did ABC Company order?
5. How does Joe Panetta solve this problem?
6. Will they cooperate in the future?

Exercise B：Listen to the conversation and fill in the blanks.

1. Our order has arrived，but you've sent the wrong ________.
2. You sent us thirteen ________ of T-shirts，fifteen ________ of trousers，and the wrong suits.
3. If you don't mind，could you tell us your ________?
4. . . . but the ________ on the ones we received is JD 5014.
5. We'll send you the right order ASAP，and give you a 10% ________.
6. I hope the ________ of trade between us will be even greater in the future.

Exercise C：Listen to the conversation and fill in the blanks.

From	
To	
Problem(s)	
How to solve it/them?	

Telephone Conversation 8

New Words and Expressions

inform *v.* 通知
tele-interview (= telephone interview) 电话面试
spare time 业余时间
digital *a.* 数字的
art exhibition 画展
a face-to-face interview 面对面面试

Caller 1: Hello, this is A College. I'd like to speak to Li Ming.
Caller 2: This is Li Ming speaking.

Caller 1: I'm glad to inform you that you've passed the entrance examination[1]. And then, I'll give you a tele-interview.
Caller 2: OK.

Caller 1: Can you introduce yourself?
Caller 2: I'm Li Ming from China. I like speaking English and studying with my friendly classmates.

Caller 1: OK, what do you do in your spare time[2]?
Caller 2: I don't have much spare time, but I like reading, listening to the music and swimming. I have a new digital camera and I like taking pictures of plants. I also like going to the cinema and I visit art exhibitions.

Caller 1: Do you think it's better to live in a small town or a big city?
Caller 2: Some people prefer big cities. It's exciting and there's a lot to do. But I don't agree with them. I live in Shanghai. I would prefer to[3] live in a smaller town, like my grandma's hometown in Shandong. Maybe it's because I like mountains.

Caller 1: All right, Li Ming, that's all. Thank you! A face-to-face interview will be arranged in the following weeks once you have passed the tele-interview successfully. Good luck! Good-bye!
Caller 2: Thank you so much! Good-bye!

Notes:

1. pass the entrance examination：通过了入学考试。
2. spare time：课余时间。
3. prefer to：更喜欢。

Exercise A：Answer the following questions.

1. Did Li Ming pass the entrance examination?
2. Where is Li Ming from?
3. What are the Li Ming's hobbies?
4. Does Li Ming like living in a big city? Why?
5. Where is his grandma's hometown?
6. What will he do once he has passed the tele-interview?

Exercise B：Listen to the conversation and fill in the blanks.

1. I'm glad to ________ you that you've passed the entrance examination.
2. I like speaking English and studying with my ________ classmates.
3. I don't have much ________ time，but I like reading，listening to the music and swimming.
4. I also like going to the cinema and I visit art ________.
5. Some people ________ big cities.
6. A face-to-face interview will be ________ in the following weeks once you have passed the tele-interview successfully.

Exercise C：Choose the following words to fill in the blanks.

in	after	back	as soon as	calling
hold the line	moment	reach	ring up	see

1. Could you ask him to call me back ________ possible?
2. Hello，who's that ________?
3. Just a ________，please.
4. I'll ________ if she's here.
5. I'll get the information you want. ________，please.
6. You asked me to ________ when I was in town again.
7. Sorry，he's not ________ at the moment.
8. You can ________ him any evening ________ six o'clock.
9. Well，I can ring ________ later if it's convenient.

Telephone Conversation 9

New Words and Expressions

distribution *n.* 销售,发送
delivery *n.* 送货
transport *v.* 运输
generally speaking 一般来说,通常
load *v.* 装载
unload *v.* 卸货
seaport *n.* 海港

Caller 1：Hello. May I speak to Benny，the distribution manager?
Caller 2：Benny speaking. Is that James?

Caller 1：Yes，this is James. How are you，Benny?
Caller 2：I'm fine，thanks. Is there anything I can do for you?

Caller 1：Yes，I would like to hear your suggestion on the delivery of our goods.
Caller 2：Well，how many goods will you transport? And what are they?

Caller 1：1,000 washing machines to Malaysia.
Caller 2：Generally speaking，we distribute a large quantity of goods to Malaysia by sea[1].

Caller 1：But you know，loading and unloading[2] will take much time at seaports. We must deliver the goods[3] before April，or else our clients won't be able to catch the shopping season[4]. Can we send them by rail?
Caller 2：By rail will be more expensive than by sea. You'll have to consider the cost，you know.
Caller 1：Oh，I see. Thank you so much.
Caller 2：You are welcome.

Notes:

1. by sea：海运。相似的如 by air(空运)/rail(铁路运输)等。

2. loading and unloading：装卸。
3. deliver the goods：发货。
4. shopping season：购物季节。

Exercise A：Answer the following questions.

1. What is the Benny's position?
2. How many goods will they deliver?
3. What disadvantage does the sea transportation mode have?
4. Why do they deliver the goods before April?
5. Which transportation mode is cheaper? By sea? Or by rail?
6. Have they come to an agreement?

Exercise B：Listen to the conversation and fill in the blanks.

1. I would like to hear your ________ on the delivery of our goods.
2. ________ washing machines to Malaysia.
3. We ________ a large quantity of goods to Malaysia by sea.
4. Loading and unloading will take much time at ________.
5. We must deliver the goods before April，or else our ________ won't be able to catch the shopping season.
6. You should ________ the costs by sea against those by rail.

Exercise C：Reading.

Now summer vacation is approaching. Lee wants to get a part-time job in a joint venture. Sam is introducing her to Michael Brown，manager of the company.

Sam： Hello，Mr. Brown. How are you?

Brown：Fine，Sam. And how are you?

Sam： I'm fine，thanks. Mr. Brown may I introduce my friend Lee to you? She is an outstanding student in our school and she speaks good English.

Lee： How do you do，Mr. Brown?

Brown：Pleased to meet you，Lee. I've heard quite a lot about you from Sam. Do you want to work for a month in my company?

Lee： I'd love to. I'd like to get a bit of real life experience. Could you offer me the chance?

Complete the following statements according to the dialogue.

1. The summer ________ is coming soon.
2. Lee wants to get a part-time job in ________.
3. Brown is ________ of the company.
4. ________ introduces Lee to Mr. Brown.
5. Lee speaks English very ________ according to Sam.
6. Sam tells Mr. Brown quite ________ about Lee.

7. Mr. Brown asks Lee if she intends to work in his company for ________.
8. Lee hopes Mr. Brown will give her ________.

Telephone Conversation 10

New Words and Expressions

travel agency 旅行社
flight *n.* 航班
book a flight 订机票
first class 头等舱
night flight 夜间航班
adult *n.* 成人
nonstop flight 直达航班

Caller 1：Good morning，Dolphin Travel Agency. What can I do for you?
Caller 2：Good morning. Well，I'd like to book a flight from Shanghai to London the day after tomorrow. What flights do you have?

Caller 1：One moment，please，and I'll find out what's available.
Caller 2：I'd like to travel first class. By the way，I don't want a night flight.

Caller 1：I see. For how many people?
Caller 2：Two adults.

Caller 1：Ok. We have a nonstop flight leaving Shanghai at 6:25 a. m.
Caller 2：No，that's too early. I want a flight after 8 a. m.

Caller 1：Both Dragon Air[1] and British Airways[2] have flights arriving at London. The Dragon Air leaves at 8:05 a. m.，and the British Airways leaves later，at 9:15 a. m. Do you have any preference?
Caller 2：Is there a British Airways?

Caller 1：Yes，there's a British Airways flight at 9:15 a. m. Would you like to make a booking?
Caller 2：Yes，please. When should I get to the airport?

Caller 1：Please be there by 8:15 a. m. at the latest.

Notes:

1. Dragon Air：港龙航空公司。
2. British Airways：英国航空公司。

Exercise A: Answer the following questions.

1. What is the customer calling to do?
2. Does the customer like a night flight?
3. Which airline does the customer choose?
4. When does the airline take off?
5. Does he make a booking?
6. When should he get to the airport?

Exercise B: Listen to the conversation and fill in the blanks.

1. I'd like to book a ________ from Shanghai to London the day after tomorrow.
2. One moment, please, and I'll find out what's ________.
3. We have a ________ flight leaving Kennedy at 6:25 a. m.
4. Both Dragon Air and British Airways have flights ________ at London.
5. Do you have any ________?
6. Would you like to make a ________?

Exercise C: Role play.

Make a short dialogue by using the useful expressions in this conversation.

Practice

I. Translate the following phrases in to Chinese.

1. be off sick
2. leave a message
3. budget figures
4. annual report
5. give a ... discount
6. advance the service
7. tele-interview
8. art exhibitions
9. a face-to-face interview
10. the entrance examination
11. prefer to
12. load and unload

13. by sea
14. a travel agency
15. first-class
16. night flight
17. a nonstop flight
18. get to

II. Fill in the blank with the phrases in Exercise I.

1. People living near the airport are pushing for new rules about ________.
2. I'd like a ________ ticket to Warsaw for this Sunday.
3. Some of the workers ________ ships.
4. Seeing that he's ________ all week, he's unlikely to come.
5. I do get a job in a ________.
6. He is reading the ________ of his company.
7. They ________ to visitors in groups.
8. Rather than travel by car, I'd ________ walk.
9. The ________ overran by fifteen minutes.
10. Is it ________ from Beijing to Los Angeles?

III. Listen to the telephone conversation and fill in the blanks.

1. Good morning, it's X ________ Inc. How can I help you?
2. This is Tom from ________ Company.
3. We know your major line is ________ ________.
4. I'd like to meet you as soon as possible and give you some ________ about our company.
5. We are especially good at ________ on line, such as B2B, B2C.
6. Thank you. Is 2 o'clock ________ for you?

IV. Role-play.

1. ABC company bought 2,500 fax machines yesterday. But when the consignment arrived, some of them didn't work. So the secretary, John, called Smith, the distribution manager. Please make a telephone conversation.
2. Making a short telephone conversation by using the following words and expressions.

leave a message	be off sick	face-to-face interview
available	travel agency	look forward

3. You cannot keep an appointment that you have made with your customer Lily Costa. Call her to *a*. apologize *b*. explain why you cannot keep the appointment *c*. suggest another date and time for the appointment.

3. Connecting and Transferring Calls *

(Telephone Conversations 11 – 15)

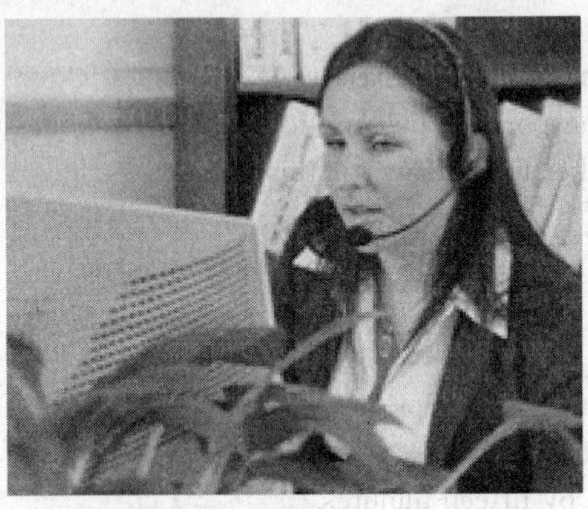

Telephone Conversation 11

New Words and Expressions
trading company 贸易公司
construction *n.* 建造,建设;建筑业
site *n.* 位置,场所,地点
by any chance 或许,可能
without fail 一定

Caller 1: Pacific Trading Company, may I help you?
Caller 2: This is Mr. Chen speaking. Could you connect me with Ms. Brown[1]?

Caller 1: Certainly, Sir. Would you hold the line a moment[2]?
Caller 2: Yes, of course.

Caller 1: Ms. Brown is on the line.
Caller 2: Hello, Ms. Brown.
Caller 3: Yes, Mr. Chen. I was waiting for your call all morning.

Caller 2: I'm so sorry, Ms. Brown. I was out at one of our construction sites and couldn't call you.

Caller 3：Now，let me see. Could you come to my office at 2 o'clock tomorrow afternoon? I'd like to discuss a few things with you then.

Caller 2：Of course，Ms. Brown. I'll be going out to another construction site tomorrow morning，so I won't be in office until noon. If，by any chance[3]，you wish to get in touch with me，could you please leave a message with my secretary?

Caller 3：Yes，I'll do that. And anyway，I'll see you here at 2 o'clock tomorrow.

Caller 2：I'll be there without fail. Goodbye，Ms. Brown.

Caller 3：Goodbye，Mr. Chen.

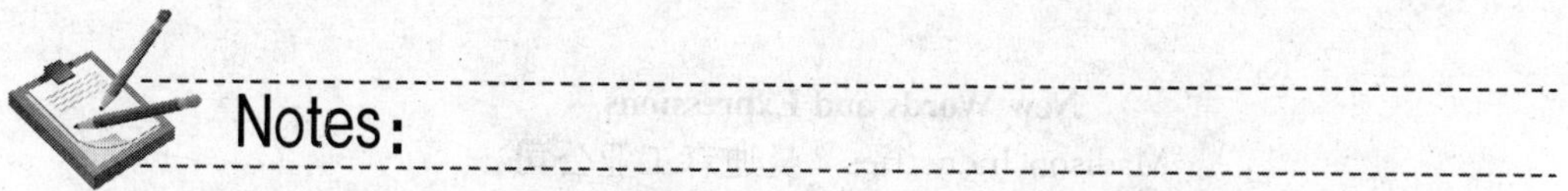

1. Could you connect me with Ms. Brown：麻烦你连线 Brown 女士，好吗？
2. hold the line：请勿收线；别挂电话。
3. by any chance：或许，可能。

Exercise A：Answer the following questions.

1. Why couldn't Mr. Chen call Ms. Brown earlier this morning?
2. Why would Ms. Brown like to meet Mr. Chen?
3. What will Mr. Chen do the next morning?
4. What will Ms. Brown do if she wants to get in touch with the Mr. Chen the next morning?
5. When will Ms. Brown meet Mr. Chen the next day?
6. Where will Ms. Brown meet Mr. Chen the next day?

Exercise B：Listen to the conversation and fill in the blanks.

1. Would you hold the line ____________?
2. Ms. Brown is on ____________.
3. I was waiting for your call ____________.
4. I was out at one of our ____________ and couldn't call you.
5. If，by any chance，you wish to ____________ me，could you please ____________ with my secretary?
6. I'll be there ____________.

Exercise C：Role play.

Ms. Brown wants to postpone the meeting with Mr. Chen to 3 o'clock due to something urgent and unexpected. Therefore，she calls Mr. Chen's secretary the next morning and leaves a message.

Telephone Conversation 12

New Words and Expressions

Madison Industries 曼迪森工业公司
corporation *n.* 公司
on behalf of 代表
general manager 总经理
without delay 立刻
assistance *n.* 协助,帮助

Caller 1: Madison Industries. This is Cathy Winer speaking. Can I help you?
Caller 2: Good afternoon. Could you connect this call with Mr. Black, please?

Caller 1: May I know who's calling?
Caller 2: This is Mary Fox of A. B. C. Computer Corporation. I'm calling on behalf of Mr. Backer, the general manager of our company.

Caller 1: I am sorry, Ms. Fox. Mr. Black is now at a meeting. May I have your number and ask him to call back later?
Caller 2: I'm afraid Mr. Baker would like to speak to Mr. Black right now. He has got an urgent matter to discuss with Mr. Black without delay.

Caller 1: OK. Then, would you please hold the line?
(*One minute later*)

Caller 1: Ms. Fox, the line is through. Mr. Black is ready to answer the call. Go ahead.
Caller 2: Thank you for your kind assistance, Ms. Winer.

Caller 1: You are welcome.

Exercise A: Answer the following questions.

1. Who is Mary Fox looking for?
2. Who is Tom Backer?
3. Is it Mr. Black available now? Why?
4. What does the receptionist suggest?
5. When would Tom Backer like to speak to Mr. Black?
6. Why would Tom Backer like to speak to Mr. Black?

Exercise B: Listen to the conversation and fill in the blanks.

1. Could you ______________________ Mr. Black, please?
2. May I have your number and ask him to ____________ later?
3. He has got an urgent matter to discuss with Mr. Black ________________.
4. Would you please ______________?
5. The line is __________.
6. Thank you for your ____________.

Exercise C: Create a follow-up telephone conversation between Mr. Baker and Mr. Black.

Telephone Conversation 13

New Words and Expressions

regarding 关于
accommodation *n.* 住宿,住处
cell phone 手机
repeat *v.* 重复
double *a.* 两个

Caller 1：Hello，this is the International Student Office. My name is Leah. How may I help you?

Caller 2：I'd like to speak to Ms. Collins，please.

Caller 1：OK. Can I ask who is calling，please?

Caller 2：This is Nathaniel Brown.

Caller 1：And what is your call regarding?

Caller 2：I'd like to talk to her about my accommodation situation.

Caller 1：OK，I'll try and put you through. Please hold on.

Caller 2：OK.

Caller 1：Sorry，her line is busy at the moment. Can I take a message?

Caller 2：Sure. Can you have her call me back on my cell phone number?

Caller 1：OK. What's your number?

Caller 2：It's 0-7-7-8-7-3-6-7-6-8-8.

Caller 1：Let me repeat that back to you. That's zero，double seven，eight，seven，three，six，seven，double six，double eight.

Caller 2：No，there's no double six at the end of the number. It's just zero，double seven，eight，seven，three，six，seven，six，double eight.

Caller 1：I got it. When should I have her call you back?

Caller 2：Anytime before 6 p. m. tonight.

Caller 1：OK，Nathaniel. I'll have Ms. Collins call you back sometime tonight before 6 p. m.

Caller 2：Thank you!

Caller 1：Bye!

Caller 2：Bye!

Exercise A：Answer the following questions.

1. Who would Nathaniel Brown like to speak to?
2. Why does Nathaniel Brown make the phone call?
3. Has the receptionist put Nathaniel Brown through? Why?
4. What does Nathaniel Brown want Ms. Collins to do?
5. What is Nathaniel Brown's cell phone number?
6. When will Ms. Collins call back?

Exercise B: Listen to the conversation and fill in the blanks.

1. Hello, this is the ______________.
2. I'd like to talk to her about my accommodation ______________.
3. Her line ____________ at the moment.
4. Can you have her call me back on my ______________?
5. Let me ____________ that back to you.
6. I'll have Ms. Collins call you back ____________ tonight before ____________.

Exercise C: Complete the following table based on what you have heard.

Caller	Nathaniel ________
Receptionist	Leah
The call is regarding	
message (detailed)	

Telephone Conversation 14

New Words and Expressions

Personnel Department 人事部
ad 广告
foreign trade 外贸
university graduate 大学毕业生
major (in) *v.* 主修，专攻
economics *n.* 经济学

frankly *ad.* 坦率地(说);老实说
experienced *a.* 有经验的
personal history statement 个人历史陈述

Caller 1：Taipei Foreign Sales Co.
Caller 2：May I have your Personnel Department，please?

Caller 1：Just a moment，please.

Caller 3：Personnel Department，Hobart speaking.
Caller 2：I'm calling about your ad in this morning's paper.

Caller 3：Oh，yes. Are you interested in doing some work in foreign trade?
Caller 2：Yes，sir.

Caller 3：May I have your name，please?
Caller 2：Tom Guo.

Caller 3：Thank you. Are you a university graduate?
Caller 2：Yes，I graduated from Taiwan University last year. I majored in economics.

Caller 3：Have you had any experience?
Caller 2：Just a little. Mostly part-time work.

Caller 3：I see. Well，frankly we're looking for an experienced person. But your English sounds pretty good. Perhaps we could train you ourselves. Could you come over to see me this afternoon?
Caller 2：Yes，sir. What time?

Caller 3：About three.
Caller 2：Yes，sir. I'll be there.

Caller 3：Please bring a copy of your personal history statement，too.
Caller 2：Yes，sir.

Caller 3：OK. I'll see you this afternoon，then. Thanks for calling.
Caller 2：Thank you.

Caller 3：Good-bye.
Caller 2：Good-bye.

Exercise A: Answer the following questions.

1. Which department was Tom Guo transferred to?
2. What is the call regarding?
3. What is Tom Guo's major?
4. How much experience has Tom Guo had in foreign trade?
5. Why would Mr. Hobart like to meet Tom Guo?
6. When will Tom Guo meet Mr. Hobart?

Exercise B: Listen to the conversation and fill in the blanks.

1. I'm ____________ your ad in this morning's paper.
2. Are you interested in ____________ in foreign trade?
3. I ____________ Taiwan University last year.
4. Have you had any ____________?
5. Frankly we're looking for a(n) ____________ person.
6. Please bring ____________ your personal history statement.

Exercise C: Make a similar dialogue.

You are a job applicant who has some working experience in foreign trade. You call Taipei Foreign Sales Co. and try to get an interview opportunity with its Personnel Department.

Telephone Conversation 15

New Words and Expressions

reservation *n.* 预定

suite *n.* 套房

standard room　标准间，标房
guest　*n.* 客人
unfortunately　*ad.* 不幸的是，不巧的是
I suppose so　我看可以

Caller 1：Hello，Pasadena Inn，this is Sandy. How may I direct your call?
Caller 2：I'd like to speak to someone about reservations.

Caller 1：I can help you with that. What date would you like to make a reservation for?
Caller 2：We'll be arriving May 12th，but I would like to make reservations for a suite.

Caller 1：Oh，I'm sorry，sir. I only handle bookings for our standard rooms. The person you need to speak with is Tony Parker. He is in charge of booking and makes all the arrangements for our guests. Unfortunately，he's not here right now. Can I take your name and number and have him get back to you?
Caller 2：When do you expect him back in?

Caller 1：He'll be out all afternoon. He might not be able to return your call until tomorrow. Will that be all right?
Caller 2：Yes，I suppose so. My name is Sam Darcy. He can contact me at 660 - 843 - 3235.

Caller 1：Could you please spell your last name for me?
Caller 2：Sure. It's D-A-R-C-Y.

Caller 1：Okay，Mr Darcy，and your phone number is 660 - 843 - 3233?
Caller 2：That's 3235.

Caller 1：Sorry! 3235. Great. I'll have Tony call you first thing tomorrow morning.

Exercise A：Answer the following questions.

1. Who would Mr. Darcy like to speak to?
2. What would Mr. Darcy like to reserve?
3. What kind of reservation does the receptionist always handle?
4. What is Mr. Darcy's full name?
5. What is Mr. Darcy's phone number?
6. When will Mr. Darcy be called back?

Exercise B：Listen to the conversation and fill in the blanks.

1. How may I ________________ your call?

2. What date would you like to ____________?
3. He ________ all the ________________ for our executive accounts.
4. When do you ________ him ____________?
5. He might not be able to ________________ until tomorrow.
6. He can ____________ me ____ 660 - 843 - 3235.

Exercise C: Writing.

Imagine you are the receptionist, and leave a note regarding the call to Tony Parker, who handles bookings for penthouses.

Practice

I. Translate the following sentences into Chinese.

1. Could you please give me the Personnel Department?
2. Would you please connect me with the Production Department?
3. Would you please transfer me to the International Division?
4. May I speak to Mr. Chen, please?
5. May I have your Sales Department, please?
6. I'll connect you.
7. I'll put you through.
8. I'll transfer you.

II. Listen to the telephone conversation and do the following exercises.

A. Answer the following questions.

1. Which company does the receptionist work for?
2. Did caller 1 speak with Miss Chen? Why?
3. Which department would Caller 2 and Caller 3 like to be connected with respectively?

B. Listen to the conversation and fill in the blanks.

1. ________ Miss Chen?
2. I'll ____ her ____ you.
3. Could you please ________ the International Division?
4. Would you please ____________ me ____ the Production Department?
5. ________________ a moment.
6. I'll ____ you ____________.

III. Role-play.

1. You are calling Far East Die Casting Corporation. You would like to speak to the manager of its Export Department, for you want to order more of their die-out gaskets（垫圈）and wonder if they can supply them at such short notice.
2. You are calling Mr. Clark to rearrange a dinner appointment with him. However, he is on

another line at the moment and you are leaving in a minute. Therefore, you leave a message with his secretary.

3. You are calling to make an appointment with your dentist. The secretary receives your call and fixes it at 3:00 p. m. Thursday.

4. Voice Mail & Taking Telephone Messages *

(Telephone Conversations 16 – 20)

Telephone Conversation 16

New Words and Expressions
detailed *a.* 详细的
tone *n.* 提示音

Hi, this is Virginia Evans. I'm sorry I cannot take your call right now. Please leave a detailed message after the tone along with your name and telephone number. I'll give you a call as soon as I return. Thank you.

Exercise A: Answer the following questions.

1. Who is the person of the voice mail?
2. Why does Virginia say that she is sorry to the caller?
3. What does she ask the caller to do?
4. What will she do after she returns?
5. What does the voice mail say in the end?
6. What kind of voice mail is it?

Exercise B: Listen to the voice mail and fill in the blanks.

Hi, this is Virginia Evans. I'm sorry I cannot take your ________ right now. Please leave a ________ message after the tone ________ with your name and ________ number. I'll give you a ________ as soon as I ________. Thank you.

Exercise C: Fill in the blanks with the information in the voice mail.

Voice Mail

person of the voice mail	
reason for apology	
the host's request	
the host's intention	

Telephone Conversation 17

New Words and Expressions

currently *ad.* 目前
unavailable *a.* 不能的
the billing department 计费部门
press *v.* 按
directory *n.* 号码簿
operator *n.* 接线员
emergency *n.* 紧急情况

Thank you for calling GNG Company. We are currently unavailable to take your call. Our business hours are nine to five, Monday through Friday. If you know the extension number of the person you are trying to leave a message for, you may dial it now. Press 1 for sales. Press 2 for customer service. Press 3 for the billing department. Press 9 for a company directory, or hold on to leave a message for the operator. If this is an emergency, please enter 911 to be connected with the after-hours support personnel[1].

Notes:

1. please enter 911 to be connected with the after-hours support personnel：请输入 911 与工作时间外支持人员取得联系。

Exercise A：Answer the following questions.

1. Why can't GNG answer the phone?
2. What are the business hours of GNG Company?
3. What can a caller do if he/she knows the extension number of the person he/she is calling?
4. What number should you press if you want to connect customer service?
5. What can you do if there is an emergency?
6. What kind of voice mail is it?

Exercise B：Listen to the voice mail and fill in the blanks.

1. Thank you for ________ GNG Company.
2. We are currently ________ to take your call.
3. Our ________ are nine to five，Monday through Friday.
4. If you know the ________ of the person you are trying to leave a ________ for，you may dial it now.
5. Press 9 for a company directory，or ________ to leave a message for the operator.
6. If this is an ________，please enter 911 now to be ________ with the after-hours support personnel.

Exercise C：Fill in the departments with the corresponding extension number according to the voice mail.

Extension Numbers of Departments

extension number	Department
1	
2	
3	
9	
911	

Telephone Conversation 18

New Words and Expressions

stay on hold 等一会儿，别挂

engage *v.* 占线

shortly *ad.* 不久，很快

Caller 1：A&D Company. This is Rosa Green speaking. How may I help you?
Caller 2：I'd like to speak with Mr. Smith, please.

Caller 1：May I ask who is speaking, please?
Caller 2：This is Paul Robert.

Caller 1：OK, Mr. Robert. Please hold while I transfer you to Mr. Smith.
Caller 2：Thank you.

Caller 1：I'm sorry, his line is busy right now. Would you like to stay on hold?
Caller 2：Sure. I can wait.

Caller 1：Alright. One moment, please ... I'm sorry, his line is still engaged[1]. Would you like to leave a message?
Caller 2：Yes, please.

Caller 1：What is your message?
Caller 2：Please tell Mr. Smith that I won't be able to make it to the interview today[2].

Caller 1：Anything else?
Caller 2：It'd be great if he could call me back this afternoon.

Caller 1：At what number shall I have him call you back?
Caller 2：You can give him my office number. It's 54308782, extension 9512.

Caller 1：So that's 54308728, extension 9512.
Caller 2：Not quite. It's 82, not 28, extension 9512.

Caller 1：Got it. I'll have him return your call shortly.
Caller 2：Thank you very much.

Notes:

1. his line is still engaged：他的线路还是占线。
2. I won't be able to make it to the interview today：我今天不能去面试了；make it：做成。

Exercise A: Answer the following questions.

1. Why does the caller call A&D Company?
2. What does Rosa ask the caller to do?
3. Why can't Mr. Robert reach Mr. David Smith immediately?
4. What does he do then?
5. What's the message about?
6. Does he leave his phone number?

Exercise B: Listen to the conversation and fill in the blanks.

1. This is Rosa Green speaking. How may I ________ you?
2. Please hold while I ________ you to Mr. Smith.
3. I'm sorry, his line is still ________. Would you like to leave a message?
4. Please tell Mr. Smith that I won't be able to make it to the ________ today.
5. It'd be great if he could ________ this afternoon.
6. I'll have him ________ your call shortly.

Exercise C: Finish the telephone message according to the conversation.

Telephone Message

To: ________________

From: ________________

Telephone No.: ________________, extension: ________________

Please call back ☐

Will call again ☐

Urgent ☐

Message: ____

____

Received by: ________________

Telephone Conversation 19

New Words and Expressions

on vacation 在度假
on duty 值班
opening *n.* 空隙;空挡
symptom *n.* 症状
gain weight 体重增加
feel sick 反胃
vomit *v.* 呕吐
confirm *v.* 确认

Caller 1：I'd like to make an appointment with Dr. Carrie.
Caller 2：He's on vacation until the 18th. Is it an emergency?

Caller 1：Yes. What other doctors are on duty today?
Caller 2：Dr. Garcia and Dr. Johnson.

Caller 1：Is Dr. Garcia available this afternoon?
Caller 2：Yes，there is an opening at 2:00.

Caller 1：That will be fine.
Caller 2：What are your symptoms?

Caller 1：I've gained some weight，I feel tired，and I often feel sick.
Caller 2：Have you experienced any vomiting?

Caller 1：Mostly in the mornings.
Caller 2：OK，I'll let him know. Can you confirm your name with me?

Caller 1：Yes，it's Michael. M-I-C-H-A-E-L. Blue. B-L-U-E.
Caller 2：And your phone number please?

Caller 1：It's 5－0－7－8－1－6－8－0.
Caller 2：So，it's Michael Blue at 50781680?

Caller 1：Yes.
Caller 2：OK，we'll see you at 2:00.

Exercise A：Answer the following questions.

1. Why is Mr. Blue calling?
2. What's wrong with him?
3. Why can't Mr. Blue visit Dr. Carrie?
4. Which doctor will Mr. Blue visit in the afternoon?
5. What's Mr. Blue's phone number?
6. When will Mr. Blue visit the doctor?

Exercise B：Listen to the conversation and fill in the form.

1. He's on vocation until the 18th. Is it an ________?
2. Is Dr. Garcia ________ this afternoon?
3. What other doctors are ________ today?
4. Ok，I'll let him know. Can you ________ your name with me?
5. Have you ________ any vomiting?
6. Ok，we'll ________ you at 2:00.

Exercise C：Finish the information of the patient and the doctors according to the conversation.

the information of the patient		
name	phone number	symptoms
		(1) (2) tired (3)
the information of the doctors		
Dr. Carrie	Dr. Garcia	Dr. Johnson
	on duty	

Telephone Conversation 20

New Words and Expressions

rainbow *n.* 彩虹
vineyard *n.* 葡萄园

shipment *n.* (运输的)货物
postpone *v.* 延迟,推迟
case *n.* 箱子
delay *v.* 延误,耽搁

Caller 1: Lipson Wine Importers. Good Morning. How can I help you?
Caller 2: Could I speak to Mr. Robert, please?

Caller 1: Who's calling please?
Caller 2: This is Jane Walker.

Caller 1: Sorry, I didn't catch your name[1].
Caller 2: Jane Walker. That's W-A-L-K-E-R.

Caller 1: Thank you. And where are you calling from?
Caller 2: Rainbow Vineyards.

Caller 1: OK Ms. Walker. I'll try and put you through . . . I'm sorry but the line's busy. Would you like to hold?
Caller 2: Could I leave a message?

Caller 1: Certainly.
Caller 2: Could you tell Mr. Robert that our shipment will be postponed and that the 300 cases ordered should arrive next Wednesday.

Caller 1: Shipment delayed . . . arriving next Wednesday.
Caller 2: Yes, and could you ask him to call me back when the shipment arrives?

Caller 1: Certainly. Could you give me your number please?
Caller 2: Yes, it's 603 - 589 - 9056.

Caller 1: That's 603 - 589 - 9056.
Caller 2: Yes, that's right. Thanks for your help. Good-bye.

Caller 1: Good-bye.

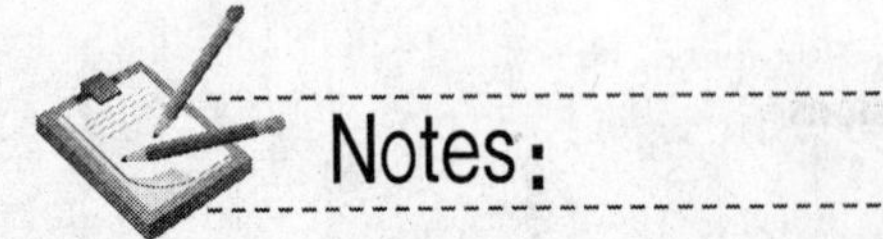

Notes:

1. Sorry, I didn't catch your name: 抱歉,我没听清你的名字。

Exercise A: Answer the following questions.

1. Which company does Ms. Walker represent?
2. Why does Ms. Walker call Lipson Wine Importers?
3. What happens to the line?
4. Why does Ms. Walker repeat her name?
5. Which information does Ms. Walker wish to leave?
6. What other information does the receptionist ask for?

Exercise B: Listen to the conversation and fill in the blanks.

1. Could I speak to ________, please?
2. Sorry, I didn't ________ your name.
3. I'm sorry but the line's busy. Would you like to ________?
4. Could you tell Mr. Robert that our ________ will be postponed and that the 300 cases ordered should ________ next Wednesday.
5. Yes, and could you ask him to call me ________ when the shipment arrives?
6. Could you give me your ________ please?

Exercise C: Fill in the blanks with the information in the conversation.

Jane Walker of Rainbow Vineyards tried to call ________ of Lipson Wine importer, but only to find that the line was ________ and he couldn't reach Mr. Robert immediately. Therefore he left a ________ to the receptionist saying that their ________ would be postponed and that the 300 cases ________ should arrive the next ________. He also left his ________ number to the ________ and asked Mr. Robert to ________ when the shipment ________.

Practice

I. Fill in the blanks with the appropriate words in the bracket.

dial	press	transfer	engage	postpone	delay
emergency	interview	symptom	shipment	case	confirm

1. She ________ for two hours and missed the train.
2. Could you carry my ________ for me?
3. You should only use this door in an ________.
4. I've got a(n) ________ with National Chemicals.
5. The match was ________ to the following Saturday because of bad weather.
6. When asked, she ________ that she was going to retire.
7. The goods are now ready for ________.
8. What happens if I ________ the reset button?
9. ________ include headaches and vomiting.
10. Put in the money before ________.

II. Listen to the telephone conversation and fill in the blanks.

1. Ellen calls Linda but Lisa tells her that she has just stepped out ________.
2. Linda offers to ________ for her, in which Ellen wants Lisa to tell Linda to ________ her at Daguangming Movie Theatre at 6:30 tonight.
3. Lisa fails to ________ because she has to take another call.
4. Lisa asks Ellen to ________ and gets what she says.

III. Role-play.

1. You want to talk to your friend, but he/she isn't at home. You leave a message for him / her.
2. Mary called you this morning, but you weren't in. she left a message for you to ring him back. Now call her.
3. You'll be out on business for two weeks. Make a voice mail for yourself.

5. Providing Information & Explanation

(Telephone Conversations 21 - 25)

Telephone Conversation 21

New Words and Expressions

visa *n.* 签证
Germany *n.* 德国
German *n.* 德语 *a.* 德国的
guidance *n.* 指南
application form 申请表
do research on 做调查
sort out 解决

Caller 1: This is ABC Student's Center. May I help you?
Caller 2: Yes. I'd like some information about studying abroad.

Caller 1: Where would you like to go?
Caller 2: I'd like to go to America, but I don't know if I can get a visa to go there.

Caller 1: Do you have any other ideas?
Caller 2: I've heard that Germany is nice.

Caller 1：Do you speak German?
Caller 2：A little，but I'm willing to learn.

Caller 1：You're right in considering different countries because of the visa. But I suggest you think about why you want to study abroad. If you want to improve your English skills，it would be best to go to a native English-speaking country. England，Canada，America and Australia are the most popular countries for studying abroad.
Caller 2：Oh. Well，can you tell me how to apply for my visa?

Caller 1：First，I think you should look into some schools and apply[1]. If you are accepted，then the universities will offer you some guidance on applying for the visa.
Caller 2：When shall I send my application forms in?

Caller 1：Over the summer，you can do some research on the schools. Then，you can send out for the application form[2] in September. Try to send them back to the school by December. That will give you plenty of time to sort out the visa[3].
Caller 2：Thanks for your help!

Caller 1：Sure thing[4].

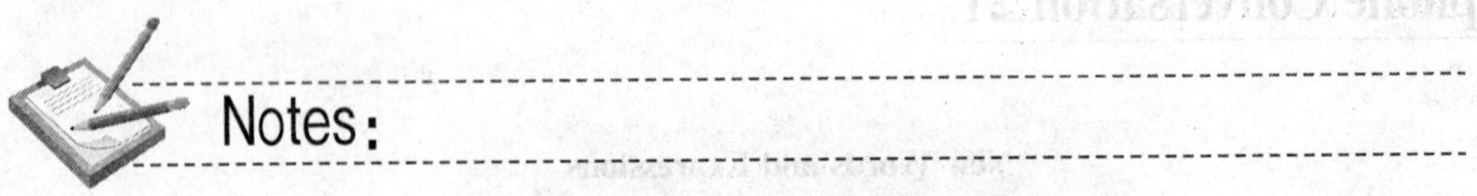

1. look into some schools and apply：找几所学校并提出申请。
2. send out for the application form：写信索取申请表。
3. That will give you plenty of time to sort out the visa：那样你就有大量时间去办签证了。
4. Sure thing：没关系。

Exercise A：Answer the following questions.

1. What organization does the caller 2 phone?
2. Why does the caller 2 make this phone call?
3. Where does he want to go?
4. Can he speak German?
5. What questions does the caller 2 ask?
6. What do you think of the receptionist?

Exercise B：Listen to the conversation and fill in the blanks.

1. I'd like to go to America，but I don't know if I can get a ________ to go there.
2. I've heard that ________ is nice.

3. You're right in ________ different countries because of the visa.
4. If you are ________, then the universities will ________ you some guidance on applying for the visa.
5. Over the summer, you can do some ________ on the schools.
6. That will give you ________ of time to sort out the visa.

Exercise C: Finish the exercise with the information in the conversation.

Procedures of Preparing for Studying Abroad

Step 1: Think about the reason for ____________________.
Choose a ____________________ country if you want to improve your English skills.

Step 2: Apply for a ____________.
(1) Look into __________ and apply ____________.
(2) Be given some guidance on applying for ____________.
(3) Do some __________ on the school over the summer.
(4) Send out for ____________________ in September.
(5) Send the application form back to school ____________________.

Telephone Conversation 22

New Words and Expressions

dishwasher *n.* 洗碗机
appliance *n.* 电器器具
microwave oven 微波炉
vacuum cleaner 吸尘器
entertainment center 家庭影院
for sale 待售,出售
speaker *n.* 扬声器

Caller 1: Hi, I'm calling about the ad in the paper. Is the dishwasher still for sale?
Caller 2: Yes, it is. Are you interested?
Caller 1: I saw the picture online and know the asking price. I was just hoping you could go down a bit in price[1].
Caller 2: Well, how about this. I have a few other things for sale. If you buy more than one appliance, I'll give you a better price.

Caller 1：What do you have?
Caller 2：I've got a microwave oven，a vacuum cleaner，and an entertainment center for sale.

Caller 1：Hmm. The entertainment center sounds interesting. Does it come with speakers[2]？
Caller 2：No，they're separate.

Caller 1：Does it work?
Caller 2：Yes. The only reason we're selling it is because we won a new one from a radio station last month.

Caller 1：Would it be all right if I came over to look at it?
Caller 2：Sure. Can you come over tonight after dinner? How about 7:00 p.m.？

Caller 1：That sounds good. And you'll think about the price[3]？
Caller 2：Of course. I'll see you then.

Caller 1：Bye!

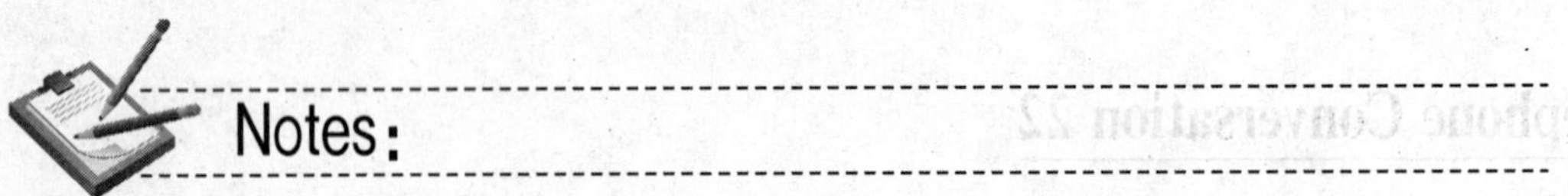

Notes:

1. I was just hoping you could go down a bit in price：我只是希望你可以降点价。
2. Does it come with speakers? 随带扬声器吗？
3. And you'll think about the price? 你会考虑再价钱便宜些？

Exercise A：Answer the following questions.

1. Where does the caller 1 get the news about things for sale?
2. What does he want to buy?
3. What other things does the store have for sale?
4. What else is he interested in?
5. What does the shop assistant promise him?
6. What does he want to do tonight?

Exercise B：Listen to the conversation and fill in the blanks.

1. I saw the picture online and know the ________ price. I was just hoping you could go down a bit in ________.
2. If you buy more than one appliance，I'll give you a ________ price.
3. The entertainment center ________ interesting.
4. The only reason we're selling it is because we ________________ a new one from a radio

station last ________.
5. Would it be all right if I ________ to look at it?
6. That sounds ________. And you'll think about the price?

Exercise C: Fill in the blanks with the information in the conversation.

The caller saw the things for sale from the ad in the paper and he was interested in the ________. Though he knew the ________ price, he still hoped Kate could ________ a bit in price. Kate said that if he would buy more than ________________, she would give him a ________________. Kate also got a ________________, a vacuum cleaner, and an entertainment center for sale. The only reason Kate was selling the ________________ was because they had won a new one from a ________________ the last month. The caller became interested in the entertainment center and decided to go over to have a look at it at ________ after ________ that night.

Telephone Conversation 23

New Words and Expressions
go on a trip 外出(旅行等)
urgently *ad.* 紧急地
bother *v.* 麻烦,打扰
depend *v.* 得看;依靠
schedule *n.* 日常安排(表)
note down 记下
diary *n.* 日记

Caller 1: Tom, here. I'm afraid I can't meet you on the day we'd planned to get together.
Caller 2: Why?

Caller 1: I have to go on a trip urgently. Would it bother you if we changed the time?
Caller 2: Well, it depends[1]. I'm actually rather busy next week. If we can't do it this Thursday, it'll have to wait until the week after next.

Caller 1: OK. Well, let me check my schedule ... I've got a meeting at 1:30 on Thursday afternoon. How about Thursday morning?
Caller 2: Yes, fine. What time exactly?

Caller 1: It depends on you.

Caller 2：I'll be free on Thursday morning. Could you come here at 8:30?

Caller 1：Yes，fine. I'll just note it down in my diary. That's Thursday morning. Right，I'll be at your place at 8:30 then，Tom.

Caller 2：OK，Mary. May you have a good trip[2].

Notes:

1. Well，it depends：嗯，那得看具体情况了。
2. May you have a good trip：祝你旅程愉快。

Exercise A：Answer the following questions.

1. Why can't Mary meet Tom on the day they'd planned to get together?
2. Which week do they change their time to?
3. What will Mary do on Thursday afternoon?
4. Will Tom be free on Thursday morning?
5. When and when will they meet?
6. What does Tom wish Mary to do?

Exercise B：Listen to the conversation and fill in the blanks.

1. I'm afraid I can't meet you on the day we'd planned to ________________.
2. If we can't do it ________________，it'll have to wait until the week after next.
3. I've got a meeting at ________ on Thursday afternoon，how about Thursday morning?
4. I'll be ________ on Thursday morning. Could you come here at ____________?
5. Yes，fine. I'll just note it down ____________.
6. ____________ you have a good trip.

Exercise C：Finish Tom's schedule according to the information in the conversation.

Tom's Schedule

this week	planned to
next week	________________
the week after next	plan again to ________________
	have a meeting ________________

Telephone Conversation 24

New Words and Expressions

rush hour 上下班高峰时间
entrance *n.* 入口
head for 往……去
Pudong International Airport 浦东国际机场

Caller 1：Dazhong Taxi Service here，can I help you?
Caller 2：Ah，yes，please. I'd like a taxi in about 20 minutes' time.

Caller 1：OK. Where are you calling from?
Caller 2：I'm at Huating Hotel. My name is Peter Brown.

Caller 1：Well，there is about a 30 minutes' wait. It's rush hour now.
Caller 2：Yes，that'll be fine.

Caller 1：Where are you headed for，Mr. Brown[1]?
Caller 2：I want to go to Pudong International Airport.

Caller 1：What is your airplane time?
Caller 2：At 11:00 a. m. I'm catching a plane to Beijing.

Caller 1：Right. Could you just wait at the entrance of the hall，sir?
Caller 2：All right. I'll be there. Let me see . . . that'll be at ten to nine.

Caller 1：Yes，OK，ten to nine. We'll be right over[2]. Good-bye.
Caller 2：Thanks，good-bye.

Notes:

1. Where are you headed for，Mr. Brown? 你要到哪里去，布朗先生？
2. We'll be right over：我们马上就到。

Exercise A：Answer the following questions.

1. Who is Peter Brown calling?

2. What does he want to do?
3. Why should he wait for 30 minutes?
4. Where is Peter Brown staying?
5. Where is Peter Brown going?
6. When will Peter Brown's plane take off?

Exercise B: Listen to the conversation and fill in the form.

1. I'd like a ________ in about 20 minutes' time.
2. Well, there is about a 30 minutes' wait. It's ________ now.
3. Where are you ________ for, Mr. Brown?
4. I'm ________ a plane to Beijing.
5. I'll be there. Let me see ... that'll be at ten to ________.
6. We'll be ________. Good-bye.

Exercise C: Finish the form according to the information in the conversation.

Name of applicant	
Hotel staying	
Destination	
Time for taxi	
Place to wait	
Airplane time	
Final destination	

Telephone Conversation 25

New Words and Expressions

reservation *n.* 预定
book a double room 订一个双人房间
extra *a.* 额外的，另加的
charge *n.* 收费

Caller 1: Advance Reservation[1]. Can I help you?

Caller 2: Yes, I'd like to change my reservation.

Caller 1: Your name, please.

Caller 2: It's Jim Carter. J-I-M C-A-R-T-E-R.

Caller 1: Yes. You've booked a double room for Mr. and Mrs. Williams from 15th to 18th.

Caller 2: Oh, yes. But the plane was late, so they won't be there on 15th.

Caller 1: And now you want to change the booking, do you?

Caller 2: Yes. Could I change my reservation from 16th to 18th?

Caller 1: Of course. Anything else, sir?

Caller 2: Yes. Actually it's for the couple and their little son, Tommy. And is there an extra charge[2] for children?

Caller 1: If the child is under sixteen and we put an extra bed[3] in their room, the charge is 10 dollars per night.

Caller 2: OK. They need an extra bed. Thank you.

1. Advance Reservation: 预订处。
2. extra change: 额外收费。
3. extra bed: 加床。

Exercise A: Answer the following questions.

1. Which section does Jim Carter call?
2. Why does Jim Carter change the reservation for Mr. and Mrs. Williams?
3. How is the reservation changed?
4. How many rooms has he booked?
5. Why do Mr. and Mrs. Williams need an extra bed?
6. How is an extra bed charged?

Exercise B: Listen to the conversation and fill in the blanks.

1. Yes, I'd like to change my ________.
2. You've ________ a double room for Mr. and Mrs. Williams from 15th to 18th.
3. But the plane was ________, so they won't be there on 15th.
4. And now you want to ________ the booking, do you?

5. And is there an extra ________ for children?
6. If the child is under sixteen and we put an ________ bed in their room, the charge is 10 dollars per ________.

Exercise C: Fill in the Guest Reservation Request according to the information in the conversation.

Guest Reservation Request

Date of arrival: ____________ Number of nights: ____________
Time of arrival: ____________ Persons: ____________
Guestroom: single ☐
double ☐

Name of applicant: ________________________________

Practice

I. Translate the following phrases into Chinese.

1. application form
2. do research on
3. sort out
4. microwave oven
5. note down
6. rush hour
7. book a room
8. for sale

II. Fill in the blanks with the phrases in Exercise I.

1. I've ________________ for you at the Majestic Hotel.
2. They are ________________ the effects of brain damage.
3. The traffic is usually very heavy during the ____________ on this road every day.
4. He sent his ____________ to the office yesterday afternoon.
5. Let me get my hands on them! I'll ________ them ________!
6. The policeman ____________ every word I said.
7. Let's go and have a look at the house ____________.
8. I bought a new ________________ for my mother.

III. Listen to the conversation and fill in the blanks.

1. Mr. Smith phones to ________________ because he has to meet someone __________ tomorrow afternoon.
2. Mr. James suggests that they meet ________________, but Mr. Smith has __________ that morning.
3. Finally they decide to meet at ________ office at nine tomorrow morning to __________ in detail.

IV. Role-play.

1. You phone an estate agent, and he is giving you some information about an estate you are interested in.
2. You are ill and you can't go class today. You are explaining your absence to your class teacher on the phone.
3. You decided to go to the cinema with your friend this evening, but something urgent happens to your family and you have to go home immediately. You are phoning your friend of canceling your appointment.

6. Delivering Messages

(Telephone Conversations 26 – 30)

Telephone Conversation 26

New Words and Expressions

represent *v.* 代表
suit *v.* 适合
book up （时间）订满
push back 推迟

Caller 1：Hello. Mr. Lee speaking.

Caller 2：Hello, Mr. Lee. This is Andrea in Mr. King's office. He wanted me to tell you that he would like to set up an appointment with you to talk about representing us in China.

Caller 1：Sure. I'd be glad to. What time suits him best?

Caller 2：He'd like to do it as soon as possible. What about tomorrow at 9 a. m. ?

Caller 1：I'm afraid I'm pretty booked up tomorrow[1]. Can we push it back to the day after tomorrow[2]?

Caller 2：Let me have a look. All right, that is no problem. What time?

Caller 1：Let's say 9 a. m. ?

Caller 2：Fine, Mr. Lee. We'll see you then.

Caller 1：See you.

Notes:

1. I'm afraid I'm pretty booked up tomorrow：明天我的时间恐怕已排满了。
2. Can we push it back to the day after tomorrow? 我们推迟到后天行吗？

Exercise A：Answer the following questions.

1. Where does Andrea work?
2. Why does Andrea phone Mr. Lee?
3. At what time would Mr. King like to meet Mr. Lee?
4. Why can't they meet at that time?
5. How do they settle the problem?
6. At what time will they meet?

Exercise B：Listen to the conversation and fill in the blanks.

1. He wanted me to tell you that he would like to ________ an appointment with you to talk about ________ us in China.
2. I'd be glad to. What time ________ him best?
3. He'd like to do it as soon as ________.
4. I'm afraid I'm pretty ________ up tomorrow.
5. Can we ________ it back to the day after tomorrow?
6. Let me have a look. All right，that is no ________.

Exercise C：Fill in the blanks with the information in the conversation.

Andrea in ________ office phones Mr. Lee to set up an ________ between Mr. King and ________ on representing them in ________. Mr. King would like to have the appointment at ________ tomorrow morning. Mr. Lee is very ________ to meet Mr. King but unfortunately he is pretty ________ tomorrow. Therefore they ________ their appointment back to the day after tomorrow and they will meet at 9 a. m. ________.

Telephone Conversation 27

New Words and Expressions

software *n.* 软件
put sb. through 接通电话
develop *v.* 开发

Caller 1：Harrison Corporation. Hi，Jane speaking.
Caller 2：Hello，I'd like to speak to Mr. Adams，please.

Caller 1：May I ask who is calling，please?
Caller 2：This is Ann Rush of Founder Computer Company.

Caller 1：Thank you，Mr. Rush. One moment，please ... (into PBX[1]) Mr. Adams，Mr. Rush of Founder Computer Company[2] is on the line.
Caller 3：Can you find out what he wants?

Caller 1：Yes，Mr. Adams. (to caller 2) I'm sorry to have kept you waiting，Mr. Rush. Mr. Adams is rather busy right now and would like to know what you wish to speak to him about.
Caller 2：Yes，I want to buy some computer software and talk about developing some other software. I don't know whether he is interested in that or not?

Caller 1：I see. Thank you very much，Mr. Rush. Would you wait a moment，please? (to PBX) Mr. Adams，Mr. Rush wants to buy some computer software.
Caller 3：I see. Put him on line two.

Caller 1：Yes，Mr. Adams. (to Caller 2) Mr. Rush，I'm very sorry to have kept you waiting. I'll put you through to Mr. Adams.

Notes:

1. PBX(Private Branch Exchange)：公司内部使用的电话业务网络(称用户级交换机)，系统内部分机用户分享一定数量的外线。
2. Founder Computer Company：方正电脑公司。

Exercise A：Answer the following questions.

1. Who is the caller 2?
2. Which organization does he call?
3. What does he want to do?
4. What does Mr. Adams ask the receptionist to do?
5. Is Mr. Adams interested in that or not?
6. What does the receptionist do finally?

Exercise B: Listen to the conversation and fill in the blanks.

1. Hello, I'd like to speak to ________, please.
2. Mr. Rush of Founder Computer Company is on the ________.
3. Mr. Adams is rather ________ right now and would like to know what you ________ to speak to him about.
4. I want to buy some computer ________ and talk about developing some other software.
5. I see. ________ him on line two.
6. I'll put you ________ to Mr. Adams.

Exercise C: Fill in the form with the information in the conversation.

Items	Mr. Adams	Ann Rush
company they belong to		
things they are doing now	being busy with his business	
purpose of phoning	becomes interested	(1) (2)
result		

Telephone Conversation 28

New Words and Expressions

conference *n.* 会议
personally *ad.* 亲自地
mobile phone 移动电话
contact *v.* 联系

Caller 1: Hello. May I speak to Mr. Green?
Caller 2: Yes, speaking.

Caller 1: Hi, Mr. Green. This is Mary. Mr. Cohen telephoned. He asked if you would be able to meet him at 4:00 p.m. today.
Caller 2: Sorry, but I'll have a conference then. Please tell me his phone number and I'll explain it to him personally.

Caller 1: Mr. Cohen said he would not be in his office this afternoon, but you can dial his mobile phone.

Caller 2: What is his mobile phone number?

Caller 1: It's 13918916161.

Caller 2: Fine. Thanks for the message. I'll contact him immediately.

Caller 1: Bye.

Exercise A: Answer the following questions.

1. Who answers Mary's phone call?
2. What did Mr. Cohen phone to do?
3. What will Mr. Green do at that time?
4. What will Mr. Green do to Mr. Cohen?
5. Where will Mr. Cohen be this afternoon?
6. How can Mr. Green contact Mr. Cohen?

Exercise B: Listen to the conversation and fill in the blanks.

1. He asked if you would be able to ________ him at 4:00 today.
2. Sorry, but I'll have a ________ then.
3. Please tell me his ________ and I'll explain it to him ________.
4. Mr. Cohen said he would not be in his ________ this afternoon, but you can ________ his mobile phone.
5. What is his ________ phone number?
6. Thanks for the ________. I'll ________ him immediately.

Exercise C: Fill in the form with the information in the conversation.

What will Mr. Green and Mr. Cohen do this afternoon?

Mr. Green	Mr. Cohen
(1) have ____________ (2) phone ____________	(1) would like to ____________ (2) not ____________

Telephone Conversation 29

New Words and Expressions

give sb. a ring 给某人打电话

estate *n.* 房产

agent *n.* 代理人
suitable *a.* 合适的
come round 顺便走访

Caller 1：Hello，Bill Johnson here.

Caller 2：Oh，Mr. Johnson，my name is Jeremy Home. You don't know me，but I'm a friend of Avid Kyd.

Caller 1：Oh，yes.

Caller 2：When I told Avid I was coming to live here he gave me your name，and suggested that I give you a ring. I was wondering if you could give me some advice.

Caller 1：I'll be pleased to if I can. What can I do for you?

Caller 2：Well，I'm looking for a place to live. Avid thought that as you're an estate agent you might know of something suitable.

Caller 1：Yes，I think I can help you. Why don't you come round and see me? Do you know where my office is?

Caller 2：Yes. I've got the address.

Caller 1：Good. Where are you now?

Caller 2：I'm at the post office.

Caller 1：Oh，well，that's just a few minutes walk from my office. Come round and see me now.

Caller 2：Thank you very much，Mr. Johnson.

Caller 1：Not at all.

Exercise A：Answer the following questions.

1. Who is Avid Kyd?
2. Where does Jeremy Home get Johnson's phone number?
3. Why is Jeremy Home phoning Mr. Johnson?
4. Where is Jeremy Home now?
5. How far is it from the post office to Mr. Johnson's office?
6. Where will Jeremy Home go?

Exercise B：Listen to the conversation and fill in the blanks.

1. You don't know me，but I'm a ________ of Avid Kyd.
2. I was wondering if you could give me some ________.

3. Well, I'm looking for a ________ to live.
4. Avid thought that as you're an estate agent you might know of something ________.
5. Why don't you ________ and see me?
6. Oh, well, that's just a few minutes walk from ________.

Exercise C:

Jeremy Home, a ________ of Avid Kyd, is coming to ________ where Mr. Johnson lives. He got Mr. Johnson's ________, address and telephone number from Avid Kyd who suggested that he give Mr. Johnson a ________. Mr. Johnson is an ________ and he can help Jeremy Home to find a ________ to live. Jeremy Home is now at the ________ and he is going to Mr. Johnson's ________ which is just a few minutes' ________ from the post office.

Telephone Conversation 30

New Words and Expressions

online *a.* 连线的,在线的

disturb *v.* 打扰

Caller 1: Hello! Is it Kumar's house?
Caller 2: Yes. May I know who's on the other end?

Caller 1: My name is Susee. I'm Kumar's friend. Can I speak to Kumar?
Caller 2: Yes. Please hold on.

Caller 2: Hello, Kumar! What are you doing there?
Caller 3: I am watching TV. Why did you call me?

Caller 2: Your friend Susee is on the line.
Caller 3: Right. Let her be online for some time. I will be there in a minute.

Caller 2: Hello, Susee! Kumar is coming. Please be online for some time.
Caller 1: OK. That is fine. I will be here waiting for Kumar.

Caller 3: Hi, Susee! How are you? What is the matter?
Caller 1: I am sorry to disturb you on Sunday. Could you come over here to meet our boss?

Caller 3: OK. I will be in our office in a few minutes.

Exercise A: Answer the following questions.

1. Where does Susee phone to?
2. Who answers the phone?
3. What is Kumar doing?
4. What does Kumar ask Susee to do?
5. Why does Susee phone Kumar?
6. What will Kumar do in the end?

Exercise B: Listen to the conversation and fill in the form.

1. May I know who's on the other ________?
2. Hello, Kumar! What are you doing ________?
3. Let her be ________ for some time. I will be there in a minute.
4. I will be here ________ for Kumar.
5. I am sorry to ________ you on Sunday. Could you come over here to meet our ________?
6. I will be in our ________ in a few minutes.

Exercise C: Fill in the blanks with the information in the conversation.

Time of calling: ________________
Relationship with Kumar: Susee: ________________
Mani: ________________
What is Kumar doing: ________________
Message delivered to Susee: ________________
Reason for Susee's calling: ________________

Practice

I. Fill in the blanks with the words or phrases in the bracket.

represent	suit	develop	contact	suitable	personally
agent	book up	push back	put sb. through	give sb. a ring	come round

1. It doesn't ________ you to have your hair cut short.
2. The hotel is fully ________, there are no more rooms available.
3. Where can I ________ you tomorrow?
4. Why don't you ________ to my flat this evening?
5. Our firm is ________ in India by Mr. Hall.
6. I'll ________ you ________ tonight.
7. The site is being ________ by a London property company.

8. If she's not in, can you ________ me ________ to her secretary?
9. The plans were ________ inspected by the minister.
10. The work was so heavy that they had to ________ the deadline.

II. Listen to the conversation and fill in the blanks.

1. Mr. Khan from Rama's ________ would like to ________ to him.
2. Sir, there is a ________ from Mr. Khan of ________ store for you.
3. All right. Please ________ him on.
4. I want an economy first class ________ to Bangalore and ________.
5. I'll ________ on that and give you a telephone call. Should I send airline ________ to your office?
6. And please bill the ________ of the tickets to Rama's store.

III. Role-play.

1. You take a message for Mary, whose friend Jane asks her to meet her at the library at 6:20 this evening. Now you are phoning to deliver the message to Jane.
2. A woman phoned to talk to Mr. Adrian Luther, but he was not in. Now you are informing Adrian Luther to call the woman back and give him the name and phone number you have taken down.
3. You are the secretary of Dr. Smith. A patient called to reschedule the appointment with Dr. Smith. Now you are phoning Dr. Smith about that.

7. Dealing with Complaints

(Telephone Conversations 31－35)

Telephone Conversation 31

New Words and Expressions

complain *v.* 投诉，埋怨
digital camera 数码相机
screen *n.* 屏幕
guarantee *n.* 保证
refund *v.* 退款
replace *v.* 更换
apologize *v.* 道歉
inconvenience *n.* 不方便，麻烦

Caller 1：NET Company. Good Morning.
Caller 2：I am making the phone call to complain about the digital camera of your company.

Caller 1：What seems to be the problem?
Caller 2：The screen always gets black.

Caller 1：Could you tell me how long this has been happening?
Caller 2：It happened about a week ago.

Caller 1：Then is the camera still under guarantee[1]？
Caller 2：Yes，I bought it only a month ago.

Caller 1：You can bring it to our repair center[2] to have it checked on first[3]. If there is some problem with the camera itself，you can have it refunded or replaced.
Caller 2：Then where is your repair center?

Caller 1：It's on the 7th Floor，1553 Palace Street. We apologize for causing you inconvenience.

Notes:

1. under guarantee：在保质期内。
2. repair center：维修中心。
3. have it checked on first：先检查一下。

Exercise A：Answer the following questions.

1. What does the man complain about?
2. What is his problem?
3. How long has the camera got the problem?
4. What does the company suggest the man doing first?
5. What will the company do if there is some problem concerning the quality?
6. Where is the repair center?

Exercise B：Listen to the conversation and fill in the blanks.

1. I am making the phone call to ____________ the digital camera of your company.
2. The screen always ________.
3. Could you tell me ________ this has been happening?
4. Then is the camera still ________?
5. You can bring it to our repair center to ____________________ first.
6. We ____________ causing you inconvenience.

Exercise C：True or False. Correct the false statements.

1. The caller made a phone call to place an order.
2. The caller bought a computer from the company.
3. The camera is still under guarantee.
4. The company refused to replace the camera.
5. The repair center is in the 7th Palace Street.

Telephone Conversation 32

New Words and Expressions

waken *v.* 叫醒;闹醒

luggage *n.* 行李

elevator *n.* 电梯

corridor *n.* 走廊

vacancy *n.* 空房,空缺(情况)

rate *n.* 价格,费用

sound *a.* (睡眠)酣畅的,深沉的

Caller 1: Good morning, reception. May I help you?

Caller 2: Yes, this is Bill Johnson in Room 1208. Can you change the room for me? It's too noisy. My wife was wakened up several times by the noise the luggage elevator made. She said it was too much for her[1].

Caller 1: I am terribly sorry, sir. I do apologize. Room 1208 is at the end of the corridor. It's likely that the noise is heard early in the morning when all is quiet.

Caller 2: Anyhow, I'd like to change our room.

Caller 1: No problem, sir. We'll manage it. Please wait a moment. I'll check the room vacancy ... How about Room 1202? It's rather quiet. The room rate is the same as that of Room 1208.

Caller 2: That's fine.

Caller 1: Then would you come to the reception to get the key to Room 1202?

Caller 2: All right.

Caller 1: If there is anything more you need, please let us know. Hope you'll have a sound sleep tonight.

Caller 2: Thank you very much.

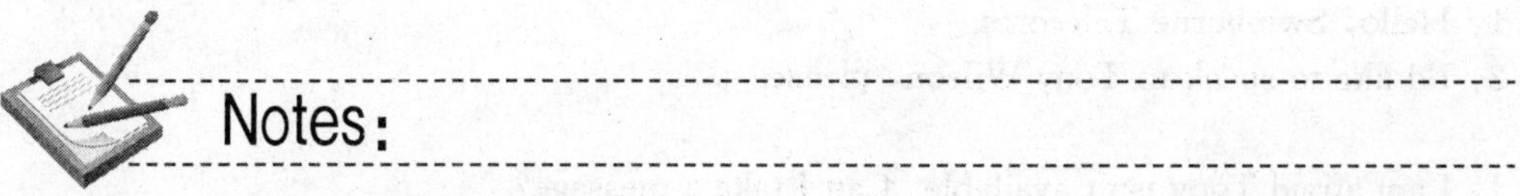

1. It was too much for her: 她受不了了。

Exercise A: Answer the following questions.

1. Who does Mr. Johnson complain to?
2. What does Mr. Johnson complain about?
3. Why is Room 1208 so noisy?
4. What's the reaction of Mr. Johnson's wife to this problem?
5. How is the problem solved?
6. What's the rate for Room 1202?

Exercise B: Listen to the conversation and fill in the blanks.

1. Can you ____________ for me?
2. She said it was ________ for her.
3. I am ________ sorry, sir.
4. It's likely that the noise is heard ____________ when all is quiet.
5. The ________ is the same as that of Room 1208.
6. Hope you'll have ____________ tonight.

Exercise C: True or False. Correct the false statements.

1. Bill Johnson couldn't stand the noise.
2. The noise was made by the vehicles outside the hotel.
3. There are no vacant rooms for Bill to change.
4. The room rate in 1202 is higher than that in Room 1208.
5. Room 1208 is at the end of the corridor.

Telephone Conversation 33

New Words and Expressions

firm *n.* 公司
install *v.* 安装
extension *n.* 分机
charge *v.* 索价，收费
instruction *n.* 操作指南，用法说明

Caller 1: Hello, Swinburne Telecoms.
Caller 2: I'd like to speak to Tony Wilson, please.

Caller 1: I am afraid Tony isn't available. Can I take a message?
Caller 2: Yes, please. I am Sheila Dallas, from WorldNet.

Caller 1：Right.
Caller 2：I am ringing about the telephone system your firm installed here yesterday. We are not happy with it.

Caller 1：Oh，dear. What seems to be the problem?
Caller 2：First of all，your engineer said that with the number of extensions we've got，six outside lines would be enough，but we asked for eight，and anyway you've charged us for the larger system.

Caller 1：Right. We'll look into that[1].
Caller 2：Then，whenever we try to transfer calls from one extension to another we lose them[2]. We are following the instructions，but it just doesn't work.

Caller 1：I see. I'm sorry about all that. I'll get Tony to contact you as soon as he's free.
Caller 2：Thank you. Good-bye.

Caller 1：Good-bye.

1. We'll look into that：我们会进行调查。
2. whenever we try to transfer calls from one extension to another we lose them：每次转分机，电话就没了。

Exercise A：Answer the following questions.

1. Who did Sheila Dallas actually want to speak to?
2. Why did Sheila Dallas make a call to Swinburne Telecoms?
3. When did the company install the telephone system for the Dallas?
4. How many telephone lines did the engineer advise the Dallas to install?
5. Why did the Dallas want to have eight telephone lines?
6. What's the second problem Sheila Dallas complained about?

Exercise B：Listen to the conversation and fill in the blanks.

1. I am afraid Tony isn't ________.
2. We are ________ with it.
3. And anyway you've ________ us for the larger system.
4. We'll ________ that.
5. We are ________，but it just doesn't work.
6. I'll get Tony to ________ you as soon as he's free.

Exercise C：Role-play.

Suppose you are Tony. Please make a call back to Sheila Dallas about her complaints.

Telephone Conversation 34

New Words and Expressions

stationery *n.* 文具，办公用品
Fennimore Consultants Fennimore 咨询公司
incorrect *a.* 不正确的，错误的
staff *n.* 员工(总称)
forward *v.* 转寄，发送
straightaway *ad.* 立即，马上
envelope *n.* 信封
pale green 浅蓝色
printer ink cartridge 打印机墨盒
assure *v.* 保证

Caller 1：Good afternoon. Stationery Supplies International，Customer Services Department，Michael speaking. How may I help you?

Caller 2：Oh，hello. My name's Jennifer Gardiner. I'm calling from Fennimore Consultants. It's about the order which we received yesterday.

Caller 1：OK. Please can I have the order number?

Caller 2：Yes，it's Z/3487/JF. The problem is we've received several incorrect items.

Caller 1：Oh dear，sorry about that. We took on some new staff this week[1] and we've had a few problems. Tell me what's wrong and we'll forward the correct order to you straightaway[2].

Caller 2：Good. Well，firstly you sent the wrong size paper. We ordered 100 boxes of A5 paper，not A4. And the envelopes you sent were not the color we ordered. We wanted pale green，not white.

Caller 1：Right，so that's A5 not A4 paper and pale green envelopes. Anything else?

Caller 2：Yes. We also ordered 20 printer ink cartridges，but you didn't send us any at all.

Caller 1：Oh dear，I'm really sorry. I can only apologize once again and assure you that the correct items will be on their way to you tonight，special delivery[3].

Caller 2：What shall I do about the things we don't want?

Caller 1：Send them back to us，and we'll refund the full cost[4].
Caller 2：Right. Thanks you. Goodbye.

Caller 1：Bye.

Notes:

1. take on some new staff this week：这星期我们雇了几名新员工。
2. we'll forward the correct order to you straightaway：我们立刻把正确的货品送上。
3. special delivery：采用特办送货方式。
4. refund the full cost：按原价退款。

Exercise A：Answer the following questions.

1. Which department answered the phone?
2. What did Jennifer Cardiner phone for?
3. What is the order number?
4. Why did the company send the wrong items?
5. How is the problem solved?
6. Who will pay for the cost when sending the incorrect items back?

Exercise B：Listen to the conversation and fill in the blanks.

1. It's about ________ which we received yesterday.
2. The problem is we've received several ________.
3. We took on ____________ this week and we've had a few problems.
4. Firstly you sent the ________ paper.
5. I can only apologize once again and assure you that the correct items will be ____________ to you tonight，special delivery.
6. Send them back to us，and we'll refund ________.

Exercise C：Read the conversation and fill in the form.

Incorrect items	Correct Items

Telephone Conversation 35

New Words and Expressions

division *n.* 部门
director *n.* 主任
query *n.* 疑问,问题
identification *n.* 辨认,识别
statement *n.* 银行结算单
debit *n.* 从账户中提取的款项
v. 将款项记入账户中的借方
odd *a.* 奇怪的,离奇的

Caller 1：Good morning. HPR Bank. Customer Services Division. How may I help you?
Caller 2：Good morning. My name's George Bliss. I'm the Financial Director[1] of Arundel Holdings. I've got a query on our business account.

Caller 1：Just a moment. I'll get it up on screen[2]. Can you give me the account number?
Caller 2：Certainly. It's 456 - 30 - 421.

Caller 1：And your identification code[3]?
Caller 2：Hamlet.

Caller 1：Right, Mr. Bliss. What's the problem?
Caller 2：Well, I received a statement from you this morning and there is a difference between that and our records. The statement shows a debit of $15,000 on June 10th, but no one here signed anything for that amount, so I'd like to know what's going on.

Caller 1：Yes, mmm, here it is - $15,000. That's odd. It says cheque number 3 - 0 - 6 - 9 - 8 - 4.
Caller 2：Yes, I can see that on the statement, but that can't be right. All our cheques begin with 5 - 0. It's not one of our cheques. You must have debited our account by mistake.

Caller 1：I am very sorry about that, Mr. Bliss. I'll sort it out immediately[4].

Notes:

1. financial director：财务主任/主管。

2. I'll get it up on screen：我将它显示在屏幕上。
3. identification code：识别码。
4. I'll sort it out immediately：我会立刻处理。

Exercise A: Answer the following questions.

1. What's the title of George Bliss in the company?
2. What is George Bliss calling to say?
3. What's George's identification code to the business account?
4. What did George find on the bank statement he received this morning?
5. What number do the cheques usually begin with in George's company?
6. How is the problem solved at last?

Exercise B: Listen to the conversation and fill in the blanks.

1. I've got a query on our ________.
2. Can you give me the ______?
3. I received a statement from you this morning and there is a ________ between that and our records.
4. It ________ cheque number 3-0-6-9-8-4.
5. You must have debited our account ________.
6. I'll ________________ immediately.

Exercise C: True or False. Correct the false statements.

1. George Bliss is the financial director of HPR Bank.
2. The caller's account number is 406-36-421.
3. The caller's bank statement is exactly the same as the records of his company.
4. The bank statement the caller received shows a debit of £15,000 on June 10th.
5. The bank debited the caller's account by mistake.

Practice

I. Translate the following phrases in to Chinese.

1. complain about
2. under guarantee
3. charge ... for
4. look into
5. take on sb
6. begin with
7. sort out
8. by mistake
9. apologize for
10. get a query on

II. Fill in the blank with the phrases in Exercise II.

1. The customer phoned to __________ the late delivery.
2. How much do you ________ a cup of coffee?
3. This company decided to ________ some new graduates.

4. Oh, sorry, I'd like to ________ not being able to attend the meeting.
5. The car is less than a year old, so it is still ________.
6. I couldn't find my briefcase. Someone must have taken it ________.
7. She is helping the secretary __________ mails and papers.
8. We'll ________ the matter immediately. Thank you for telling us.

III. Listen to the following conversation and fill in the blanks.

1. John bought a ______ yesterday, but it doesn't ________ at all.
2. The staff advised that John ________ to the company for a check or they send a ________ to John's home.
3. John preferred ________.

IV. Role Play.

Work in pairs. A is working in the Sales Department of Tao Loon Company. A received a call from the customer B complaining that the printer he bought three months ago had broken down for a fourth time. A suggested B take the printer to the repair center for a check first and promised B to refund him or replace the printer if there is something wrong with the printer itself.

Unit 2

Making Calls

1. Completing Simple Business Tasks *

(Telephone Conversations 36 - 40)

Telephone Conversation 36

New Words and Expressions

cookware *n.* 炊具
display *v.* 展示,陈列,展览
reference *n.* (方便查询的)编号,标记,索引
saucepan *n.* 炖锅,长柄而有盖子的深平底锅
mixture *n.* 混合,混合物
stainless steel 不锈钢
payment *n.* 支付,付款

Caller 1：Hello. This is Sky TV-Shopping. Can I help you?
Caller 2：Yes，I'm interested in the cookware being displayed on TV now，and I'd like to order it. I want to know some information about it.

Caller 1：Yes，madam. Could you please tell me the reference number[1] of the product?
Caller 2：It's CF19171.

Caller 1：Let me see. It's a set of German cookware. What do you want to know about it?
Caller 2：What are the two saucepans made of ? Iron or a mixture of different metals?

Caller 1：They're all made of stainless steel[2].
Caller 2：I see，and the price shown is ...

Caller 1：It's £ 355 and now any customer who buys it will get a free gift.
Caller 2：Oh，what is that?

Caller 1：It's a set of knives with a bamboo block[3].
Caller 2：That's great. Will you take the order down[4] ?

Caller 1：Sure. Would you give me your name and the address，then?
Caller 2：Yes，it's Mary Wilson of 113 Gifford Street，London.

Caller 1：Sorry，madam. I didn't catch your address. Could you please repeat it?

Caller 2：OK. It's 113 Gifford Street，London. How should I pay for it? Credit card or cash?

Caller 1：You can choose cash on delivery[5] or online credit card payment.

Caller 2：Cash on delivery. When can I expect it?

Caller 1：It should reach you within three workdays ... em ... before August 25th. Please let us know if it doesn't.

Caller 2：OK. Thanks. Goodbye.

Caller 1：Goodbye. Thanks for calling.

Notes:

1. reference number：编码。
2. stainless steel：不锈钢。
3. bamboo block：竹制砧板。
4. Will you take the order down? 能请你记一下订单吗？
5. cash on delivery：货到付款。

Exercise A：Answer the following questions.

1. Where did the caller see the product?
2. What product was the caller interested in?
3. What kind of gift can the caller get if he buys the product?
4. Where did the caller live?
5. How did the caller pay for the product?
6. When can the caller expect to get the product?

Exercise B：Listen to the conversation and fill in the blanks.

1. I'm interested in the cookware ____________ on TV now.
2. What are the two saucepans made of ? Iron or a mixture of ________________?
3. Now any customer who buys it will get ____________.
4. I ________________ your address.
5. You can choose cash on delivery or ________________ payment.
6. It should reach you within ____________.

Exercise C: Read the conversation and fill in the form.

Information about the Cookware	
Reference Number	
Made in	
Made of	
Price	

Telephone Conversation 37

New Words and Expressions

run *v.* 进行，延续

brochure *n.* 小册子

certificate *n.* 证书

familiar *a.* 熟悉的

Caller 1: Good morning. Oakleaf Business Training. How can I help you?

Caller 2: Hello, my name is Enid Smith. I've booked two one-day courses, but now I need to change one of them.

Caller 1: Let me get your details up on the screen[1]. Right, you've booked Report Writing next month ...

Caller 2: Yes, that one's OK. It's Taking Minutes that I can't manage, on the 8th of July. Do you know when it's running again?

Caller 1: Let me see. Not until the 18th of September, I am afraid.

Caller 2: That sounds fine. Oh, I think I'll be abroad then.

Caller 1: Then there is the first and the thirteenth of October.

Caller 2: I'd like the later date, please.

Caller 1: Fine, I'll change your booking.

Caller 2: Another thing, it says in your brochure, everyone attending a course gets a certificate[2], but I haven't received one from a course I took last January.

Caller 1：I am sorry about that. Which course was it?
Caller 2：Something to do with dealing with[3] the public . . . ?

Caller 1：That must have been Customer Service.
Caller 2：Sounds familiar.

Caller 1：OK，I'll put it in the post today[4].
Caller 2：Thank you very much. Good-bye.

Caller 1：Good-bye.

Notes:

1. Let me get your details up on the screen：让我把你的信息在屏幕上显示出来。
2. everyone attending a course gets a certificate：凡参加课程培训的人均将获得一份证书。
3. deal with：与……打交道。
4. I'll put it in the post today：我今天就把它邮出去。

Exercise A：Answer the following questions.

1. Why did Enid Smith make the call?
2. How many courses has Enid Smith booked?
3. Which course can Enid Smith manage to attend?
4. When did Enid Smith decide to attend the course Taking Minutes at last?
5. What does the Training center promise in the brochure for whoever attend a course?
6. Which course did Enid Smith attend last January?

Exercise B：Listen to the conversation and fill in the blanks.

1. I've ________ two one-day courses.
2. Let me get your ________ up on the screen.
3. Do you know when ____________ again?
4. I'd like the __________，please.
5. Another thing，it says in your brochure，everyone ______________ gets a certificate.
6. I'll put it __________ today.

Exercise C：Fill in the blanks according to the dialogue.

Enid Smith has booked two ___________ in Oakleaf Business Training. One is Report Writing which starts ____________；the other is Taking Minutes that is on the eighth of _______. Due to some reason，she couldn't attend the course of _______. Thus she made a call to Oakleaf Business Training to __________. She was told the course would run again on ______________ different times. Finally, Enid Smith chose to attend the course on the __________.

Telephone Conversation 38

New Words and Expressions

rental *a.* 租用的，出租的
mini-van *n.* 面包车
sedan *n.* 小轿车
gasoline *n.* 汽油
reserve *v.* 保留
agreement *n.* 协议(书)

Caller 1：JFK Airport Car Rental Service. How can I help you?
Caller 2：This is Angel Tan. I am arriving at JFK[1] on the 22nd of April. I'd like to rent a car.

Caller 1：Sure. How many days do you want the car，Ms. Tan?
Caller 2：Let me see. I'm flying back on the 25th ... so three days.

Caller 1：OK. And what kind of car would you like?
Caller 2：Well，I don't really know American cars ... I'll be in the States[2] on business[3]. I need a car that I can take customers in.

Caller 1：Well，we have mini-van available with a driver if you need ...
Caller 2：Oh no. I don't need anything that big. Just a four door sedan is fine.

Caller 1：How about a Nissan Maxima[4]?
Caller 2：That's fine. How much is it?

Caller 1：$95 per day，plus gasoline. Do you want me to reserve it for you?
Caller 2：Yes，please.

Caller 1：OK. And can I have your fax number? I'll fax you a form to fill in and the details of the rental agreement[5].
Caller 2：Sure. May fax number in Singapore is 2563 298.

Caller 1：That's 2563 298. Thank you Ms. Tan. Bye.
Caller 2：Thank you. Good-bye.

Notes:

1. JFK：美国肯尼迪国际机场(John F. Kennedy International Airport)。
2. in the States：等于 in the United States。
3. on business：出差。
4. Nissan Maxima：日产汽车的一个品牌，直译为玛西玛。
5. rental agreement：租借协议。

Exercise A：Answer the following questions.

1. Why did Angel Tan make a call?
2. When will Angel Tan arrive at the JFK airport?
3. Why will Angel Tan need a car in the States?
4. What kind of car does Angel Tan prefer?
5. How much is it to rent a car?
6. What will be sent to Angel Tan by fax?

Exercise B：Listen to the conversation and fill in the blanks.

1. I'd like to ________________.
2. I'm ________ on the 25th.
3. I'll be in the States ________.
4. We have mini-van available with ________ if you need . . .
5. How much is it? $95 per day, ________ gasoline.
6. I'll fax you a form to fill in and ________ of the rental agreement.

Exercise C：Fill in the blanks according to the dialogue.

Angel Tan works in ________. She will have a ________ to America from April the 22nd to the 25th. In order to receive ________, she made a phone call in advance to JFK Airport Car Rental Service to rent a car. The staff recommended a mini-van ________ with a driver, but Ms. Tan prefers a ________ sedan. At last, she reserved a Nissan Maxima at ________, plus gasoline. To confirm her reservation, she has to fill in ________________ and sign a ________________ sent by ________ from the JFK Airport Car Rental Service.

Telephone Conversation 39

New Words and Expressions

update *v.* 为……提供最新信息
seminar *n.* 研讨会
location *n.* 位置，场所
buffet *n.* 自助餐
sort *n.* 种类，类别

Caller 1：Good morning. Rachel Bould's office. Can I help you?

Caller 2：Good morning. This is Janet Shibuya here, from the Conference Reservation Service. Can I speak to Rachel?

Caller 1：I'm afraid she's out of the office. Would you like to leave a message?

Caller 2：Sure. I just wanted to update her on the booking for your Management Seminar on the 24th of April.

Caller 1：Oh yes. At the Russell Hotel.

Caller 2：Well, no, that's what I'm phoning about. I wasn't able to get the Russell hotel. They were fully booked. But I've got you in at the Tower Hotel. That's in the centre of London too. The location is very convenient.

Caller 1：And what about the price?

Caller 2：Well, the basic price is the same. The good thing is that now you have the choice of a buffet lunch or a full restaurant meal[1]. The buffet lunch is cheaper, so would you like to go for[2] that?

Caller 1：I'll ask Mrs. Bould about that and let you know.

Caller 2：Right. Then the other thing is, could you send me a list of the equipment you'll be needing — OHP[3], video ... that sort of things.

Caller 1：Can we get back to you on that one by Friday[4]?

Caller 2：That'll be fine.

Notes:

1. a full restaurant meal：一顿丰盛的大餐。
2. go for：选择，挑选。
3. OHP：高射投影仪（= Overhead Projector）。
4. Can we get back to you on that one by Friday? 关于这一点我们星期五再说行吗?

Exercise A：Answer the following questions.

1. Who would Janet Shibuya like to speak to?
2. What did Janet Shibuya phone for?
3. What will be held on the 24th of April?
4. Why can't the seminar be held at the Russell Hotel?
5. What hotel did Janet get instead?
6. What are the attractive points the alternative hotel has got?

Exercise B：Listen to the conversation and fill in the blanks.

1. Would you like to ________________?
2. I just wanted to ________ her on the booking for your Management Seminar on the 24th of April.
3. They were ________ booked.
4. That's in the centre of London too，the ____________ is very convenient.
5. The good thing is that now you __________________ of a buffet lunch or a full restaurant meal.
6. Could you send me ____________ the equipment you'll be needing — OHP，video ... that sort of things.

Exercise C：True or False. Correct the false statements.

1. Janet Shibuya made a call to Rachel about private affairs.
2. The seminar will be held at the Tower Hotel at first.
3. The price of the Russel Hotel is much higher than that of the Tower Hotel.
4. The Tower Hotel offers a cheaper buffet lunch and a full restaurant meal.
5. Janet also wants Mrs. Bould to provide a name list of the guests attending the seminar.

Telephone Conversation 40

New Words and Expressions

property *n.* 财产,房地产
range *n.* 范围,幅度
specific *a.* 具体的,明确的
facility *n.* 设施
definitely *ad.* 肯定的,确定的

Caller 1: Rental Property Management. Jane speaking. How may I help you?
Caller 2: This is Iris. I'd like to rent a two-bedroom apartment.

Caller 1: OK. In order to meet your needs better, I would like to ask you a few questions. First, what price range[1] are you interested in?
Caller 2: Somewhere between \$400 and \$500 a month.

Caller 1: Did you have a specific location in mind?
Caller 2: Well, I would like to live somewhere near my company, or at least on a bus line[2].

Caller 1: And when would you like to move in?
Caller 2: On the first of next month.

Caller 1: OK. Are there any other facilities which you would like to have? For example, a washing machine, a refrigerator or central air conditioning?
Caller 2: I would definitely like to have a washing machine, a refrigerator and with summers like these, central air conditioning[3]! Oh, yes, two bathrooms would be nice.

Caller 1: OK. We have one apartment on Huaihai Road that meets your requirements.
Caller 2: Good. Can I go and have a look at it?

Caller 1: Sure. What time will suit you best?
Caller 2: I am available this Sunday afternoon.

Caller 1: Then let's go and see it on Sunday afternoon. Say, 2:00 p.m.?
Caller 2: Great. See you then.

Notes:

1. price range：价格范围。
2. at least on a bus line：至少在同一公交线上。
3. ... and with summers like these，central air conditioning！像这么热的夏天，当然最好有中央空调！

Exercise A：Answer the following questions.

1. What kind of apartment does Iris want to rent?
2. What price range can Iris afford?
3. Where does Iris want to rent the apartment?
4. When does Iris prefer to move into the new apartment?
5. What facilities does Iris would like to have?
6. When will Iris and the staff go to see the apartment on Huaihai Road?

Exercise B：Listen to the conversation and fill in the blanks.

1. I'd like to rent a ____________________.
2. What ____________ are you interested in?
3. Did you have a specific location ________?
4. I would like to live somewhere near my company，or at least on ________.
5. We have one apartment on Huaihai Road that ____________________.
6. What time will ________ you best?

Exercise C：True or False. Correct the false statements.

1. Iris called to buy a house.
2. Iris prefers that the price of the apartments is below $500.
3. Iris doesn't care where the apartment is.
4. Iris wants to move into the new apartment at the beginning of next month.
5. There are not any appropriate apartments that meet Iris' requirements now.

Practice

I. Translate the following phrases in to Chinese.

1. reference number
2. cash on delivery
3. deal with
4. update sb on sth
5. put ... in the post
6. on business
7. rental agreement
8. price range
9. get back to sb
10. have ... in mind

II. Fill in the blank with the phrases in Exercise I.

1. He is going ________ in Spain, so he couldn't attend the meeting.
2. Do you ________ a proper candidate ________ for the post of General Manager?
3. Sorry, Mr. Clark is busy now, he said he would ________ you on the final decision later.
4. You are required to offer the ________ of the items if you want to order something online.
5. Would you help ________ this parcel ________ later?
6. I couldn't afford this car. It was out of my ________.
7. The two books both ________ the Chinese history.
8. I will ________ the Board ________ our progress after the meeting.

III. Listen to the following conversation and fill in the blanks.

1. The caller called to book a ________ room for a guest for ________ nights.
2. The hotel charged ________ for a room per night.
3. The guest will check in at the hotel on ________ at last.

IV. Role-play.

You are John Rees of Heiwa Life Insurance. Make a call to Industrial Air Conditioning Limited and ask them to send you a brochure for office air conditioners.

2. Completing More Complicated Business Tasks *

(Telephone Conversations 41 - 45)

Telephone Conversation 41

New Words and Expressions

depot *n.* 库房,仓库
catalogue *n.* 目录
laptop *n.* 手提电脑
briefcase *n.* 公文包
reclining *a.* 斜倚的,斜靠的
alarm clock 闹钟

Caller 1: Office Depot[1], Catalogue Sales[2]. May I help you?
Caller 2: Yes. I'd like to place an order[3].

Caller 1: Certainly. Your customer number, please?
Caller 2: 324678.

Caller 1: Right. Now, Mr. Evans, if you'd like to give me the item number and item description[4], please.
Caller 2: OK. First, I'd like to order item 4532. That's the Toshiba 2100 laptop with the black case.

Caller 1: Right.
Caller 2: Next, I'd like the brown briefcase, item number 11437.

Caller 1: Brown ... briefcase ... 11437. Anything else?
Caller 2: I'd like item 6709, and I want it in red, please.

Caller 1: All right. That's the reclining office chair[5].
Caller 2: That's right. Next, number 2362, the Seiko alarm clock.

Caller 1: 2362 ... Seiko alarm clock. That's great. Oh, one second, what colour alarm clock do you want? It's available in grey or blue[6].
Caller 2: Hmm ... grey, I think. Yes, grey.

Caller 1: Great. You can expect to receive your order within a week[7].
Caller 2: That's fine. Thank you.

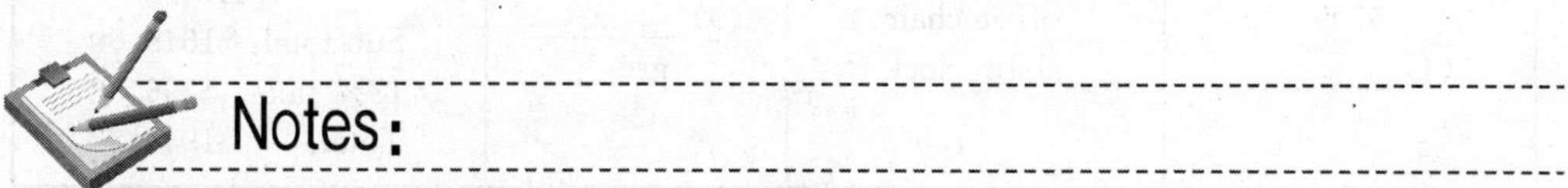

1. Office Depot：供货仓库。
2. Catalogue Sales：目录销售。这是一种新的销售方式,即客户按公司制定的商品分类目录(经常是图文并茂的)下单,不必去供货现场。
3. place an order：下订单。
4. item description：商品描述。
5. reclining office chair：可斜仰的办公椅。
6. It's available in grey or blue：它有灰色和蓝色的。
7. You can expect to receive your order within a week：你可望在一周内收到订单。

Exercise A: Answer the following questions.

1. Why did the caller make the phone call?
2. What is the caller's customer number?
3. How many items did the caller order?
4. Which two things does the caller have to offer if he wants to place the order?
5. When can the caller receive his order?
6. What is it for the item number 11437?

Exercise B: Listen to the conversation and fill in the blanks.

1. I'd like to ________________.
2. If you'd like to give me the item number and __________, please.

3. That's the Toshiba 2100 laptop with the ________.
4. I'd like item 6709, and I want it ________, please.
5. It's ____________ in grey or blue.
6. You can ________ receive your order within a week.

Exercise C: Here is the customer's receipt. Please fill in the blank with the missing information according to the conversation.

Office Depot plc			**Catalogue Sales — Customer Receipt**	
Customer Number: 324678 Date of order: Feb. 14, 2012				Shipping date: Feb. 19, 2012
Qty	**Item Number**	**Item Description**	**Colour**	**Price**
1 1 1 1	4532 (2) ________ 6709 (4) ________	(1) ________ briefcase office chair alarm clock	black brown (3) ________ grey	$1500 $89 $42 $18 Sub total: $1649.00 18% tax: $296.82 Total: $1945.82

Telephone Conversation 42

New Words and Expressions
deal *n.* 交易，买卖
commercial *n.* 电视广告
stock *n.* 库存
goods *n.* 商品，货物
model *n.* 型号，模型

Caller 1: Hello, Pioneer Trading Company. Jerry speaking.
Caller 2: Hello, this is Steve from ABC Company. May I speak to Mr. Clark?

Caller 1: Hold on, please. I'll put you through.
Caller 2: Thank you.

Caller 3: Hello, this is Clark. Can I help you?

Caller 2：Hello，it is Steve from ABC Company. Here is the deal；we wish to place an order with your corporation for 1，000 computers. Do you have in stock[1] any new models that are shown on your TV commercial?

Caller 1：Yes，we have enough goods to meet your needs. We can provide more than 5，000 computers，if you like.

Caller 2：Actually，it is more than we need. You're asking too much for it.

Caller 1：And we can offer you computers in different levels of quality[2]. You can take a little cheaper model.

Caller 2：How many different models of this do you offer?

Caller 1：We have five different ones.

Caller 2：Is there much of a difference in price[3]?

Caller 1：Yes，the economy model is about 30% less.

Caller 2：But your prices still seem a little high.

Caller 1：You could save a lot if you would order a little more. We offer a discount for large orders[4].

Caller 2：All right，I'll think it over. Thank for your help. I'll call you back later.

Caller 1：My pleasure.

Notes:

1. in stock：有存货，有现货。
2. in different levels of quality：不同质量等级。
3. Is there much of a difference in price? 价格差别大不大？
4. We offer a discount for large orders：我们为大量订货提供折扣。

Exercise A：Answer the following questions.

1. Who transferred the call to Mr. Clark?
2. What did Steve call for?
3. Where did Steve see the new model of this computer?
4. How many different models of this computer does the company offer?
5. What does the caller think of the price of the economy model?
6. What did the caller decide to do at the end of the calling?

Exercise B: Listen to the conversation and fill in the blanks.

1. I'll put you ________.
2. Do you have any ________ on your TV commercial in stock.
3. Yes, we have ________ to meet your needs.
4. You can take ________ model.
5. Is there much of ________ in price?
6. We offer a discount for ________.

Exercise C: True or False. Correct the false statements.

1. Steve made a call to Mr. Clark directly.
2. Mr. Clark was out of the office and thus didn't answer the call.
3. The caller wanted to order 1,000 computers from ABC Company.
4. The caller thought the price for the new model of this computer was reasonable and acceptable.
5. The company can offer a discount for large orders.

Telephone Conversation 43

New Words and Expressions

schedule *v.* （时间上）计划，安排
cancel *v.* 取消
unit *n.* 单元；部件

Caller 1: Hello. Can I speak to Sam Wong?
Caller 2: May I have your name, please?

Caller 1: This is Bob Black from Planning Department.
Caller 2: Hold on, please ... I'm sorry, but he's on another line now. Would you care to hold?

Caller 1: Well, I need to leave in a minute. Could you take a message, please?
Caller 2: Certainly.

Caller 1: It's about the meeting we scheduled for Wednesday.
Caller 2: Oh yes, about the new factory site ...

Caller 1: That's right. I've just heard from the builder that he can't come on Wednesday. I wonder if we can change the date[1].

Caller 2: That shouldn't be a problem. I'll just look in Mr. Wong's diary. Right, I've cancelled Wednesday's meeting.

Caller 1: OK, now how's he fixed on Friday[2]...?

Caller 2: He's got a meeting at nine-thirty but that should be finished by ten-fifteen. What time did you have in mind?

Caller 1: Well, the two of us can come any time that morning, so could we make it 11 o'clock[3]?

Caller 2: That sounds fine.

Caller 1: We want to discuss the new production units[4], so could you ask Sam to bring his plans with him.

Caller 2: Yes, certainly.

Caller 1: Thanks a lot, Good-bye.

Caller 2: Good-bye.

Notes:

1. I wonder if we can change the date：我正想你能否将日子变动一下。I wonder...系一种客套的表达方法，常用于征求意见。
2. How's he fixed on Friday? 他周五有什么安排？
3. ... so could we make it 11 o'clock? 我们能不能把它定在 11 点？用 could 比用 can 更为客气。
4. production units：生产单元。

Exercise A: Answer the following questions.

1. What department does Bob belong to?
2. Why wouldn't Bob like to wait for Sam Wong to finish another calling?
3. What did Bob call for?
4. What is their meeting about?
5. What's Sam Wong's schedule on Friday?
6. When did Bob finally decide to come to meet Sam Wong on Friday?

Exercise B: Listen to the conversation and fill in the blanks.

1. I'm sorry, but he's ________________ now.
2. Would you ________ hold?
3. It's about ________ we scheduled for Wednesday.

4. I've just heard from ________ that he can't come on Wednesday.
5. So could we ________ 11 o'clock?
6. Could you ask Sam to bring ________ with him.

Exercise C: Fill in the blanks according to the dialogue.

Bob Black Works in Planning Department. He planned to have ________ with Sam Wong about the new factory site on ________. But he got news that ________ couldn't come to attend the meeting that day. Therefore, Bob made a phone call to ________ and hoped to change the date for the meeting. Unfortunately, Sam Wong was ________ another phone call. Then Bob asked the secretary to take ________ for Sam Wong and decided on another time to have the meeting on ________.

Telephone Conversation 44

New Words and Expressions

purchasing *n.* 采购,购买
packaging *n.* 包装
machinery n.(总称)机器
term *n.* (协议、合同等)条款,条件
penalty *n.* 惩罚,处罚
clause *n.* (法律文书的)条款
waive *v.* 放弃(权利、要求等)
bulk *n.* 大宗,大批(买卖)
maintenance *n.* 维修,保养
installation *n.* 安装

Caller 1: Hello. Could I speak to Bob Cole in Purchasing, please?
Caller 2: I'm afraid he's out of the office for the day. Can I take a message?

Caller 1: Yes, Please. It's Alex Parker from Pilton Engineering.
Caller 2: Oh yes. We ordered some packaging machines from you, didn't we?

Caller 1: That's right, but I'm going to have to postpone the delivery date. We're having problems finding the right lifting machinery[1] for them.
Caller 2: I see.

Caller 1: Now, under the terms of the contract[2] I signed, there is a penalty clause for late delivery[3]. But I'm hoping Bob will waive that, since I also agreed to very good bulk discount[4].

Caller 2: I'll check for you.

Caller 1: Thanks. I've decided that, as we're doing the maintenance, I won't charge for installation.

Caller 2: OK. I've got that.

Caller 1: Oh, and one more thing-I can't find anything in the contract about who's dealing with insurance while the goods are on the road.

Caller 2: I'll check that.

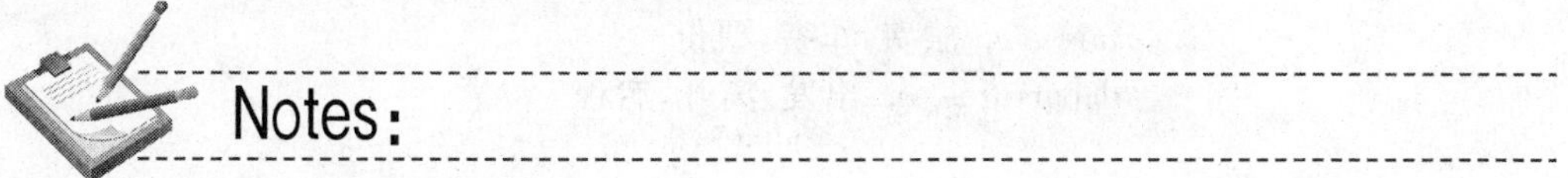

Notes:

1. lifting machinery：起重机器。
2. under the terms of the contrat：根据合同条款。
3. a penalty clause for late delivery：一项关于推迟交货的惩罚条款。
4. very good bulk discount：极为优惠的大单折扣。

Exercise A: Answer the following questions.

1. What department is Bob Cole from?
2. What was ordered from the caller's company?
3. Why did the caller phone to postpone the delivery date?
4. What is said about late delivery according to their contract?
5. What did the caller promise if Bob wouldn't mind the late delivery?
6. What will the caller not charge for when they are doing the maintenance?

Exercise B: Listen to the conversation and fill in the blanks.

1. We ordered some ____________ from you, didn't we?
2. But I'm going to have to postpone the ____________.
3. We're having ________ finding the right lifting machinery for them.
4. But I'm hoping Bob will waive that, since I also ________ very good bulk discount.
5. I've decided that, as we're ________________, I won't charge for installation.
6. I can't find anything in the ________ about who's dealing with ________ while the goods are on the road.

Exercise C: True or False. Correct the false statements.

1. Alex Parker works in the Purchasing of Pilton Engineering.
2. Some lifting machines were ordered from the caller's company.

3. The caller wanted to postpone the delivery because of the weather.
4. Bob Cole didn't mind the late delivery.
5. The caller knows clearly who's dealing with insurance while the goods are on the road.

Telephone Conversation 45

New Words and Expressions

agency *n.* 代理,经销,代理机构
airline *n.* 航空公司
fare *n.* 旅费,车费,票价
departure *n.* 出发,离开,启程

Caller 1：Travel Agency. May I help you?
Caller 2：I'd like to make a plane reservation from Shanghai to London.

Caller 1：You name, please.
Caller 2：Jason Lopez. I'd like to leave on August 28th.

Caller 1：Could you spell your name please?
Caller 2：That is J-A-S-O-N L-O-P-E-Z.

Caller 1：Thank you. Let me see what's available ... yes, China Airlines has a flight on August 28th. How do you want to fly, an economy class or first class?
Caller 2：I need an economy ticket.

Caller 1：One way trip[1] or round trip[2]?
Caller 2：Round trip, please. What's the fare please?

Caller 1：Economy fare for round trip from Shanghai to London is $1,600.
Caller 2：Is my ticket confirmed then?

Caller 1：Yes. Please arrive at the airport one hour before departure.
Caller 2：May I have the flight number, please?

Caller 1：Your flight number is CA 981. It leaves Shanghai Pudong International Airport at 3:00 p.m. on August 28th. OK, you are all set[3], Mr. Lopez. Enjoy your flight.
Caller 2：Thanks.

Notes:

1. one way trip：单程旅行。
2. round trip：往返旅行。
3. You are all set：你的办好了/完成了。

Exercise A：Answer the following questions.

1. What was Mr. Lopez calling for?
2. When did Mr. Lopez want to leave for London?
3. Which airline has the proper flight for Mr. Lopez?
4. What kind of ticket did the caller choose?
5. How many hours should Mr. Lopez arrive at the airport before departure?
6. Which airport will Mr. Lopez check in?

Exercise B：Listen to the conversation and fill in the blanks.

1. I'd like to ____________ from Shanghai to London.
2. Let me see ____________.
3. How do you want to fly, an ________ or ________?
4. Economy fare for ____________ from Shanghai to London is $1,600.
5. Please arrive at the airport one hour before ________.
6. OK, you are ________, Mr. Lopez. Enjoy your flight.

Exercise C：Please fill in the flight information according to the dialogue.

Airlines	
Name	
Flight Number	
Flight Date	
Class	
Fare for a Round Trip	
Destination	

Practice

I. Translate the following phrases in to Chinese.

1. place an order
2. put sb through
3. in stock
4. hear from

5. under the terms of
6. a penalty clause
7. bulk discount
8. round trip
9. first class
10. think over

II. Fill in the blank with the phrases in Exercise I.

1. We wish to ________ with your corporation for 10,000 bicycles.
2. They have plenty of stonewashed jeans ________.
3. We hope to ________ your company soon.
4. I suggest you ________ your position very carefully.
5. Hold on, please. The operator will ________ you ________.
6. If your order is large, we would offer you a ________.
7. You can buy a ________ ticket. It saves you about 15% of the fare.
8. ________ the agreement, you have to pay a weekly rent.

III. Listen to the following conversation and fill in the blanks.

1. Elizabeth Parnell called to postpone Wednesday's meeting till ________ because she would only get back on Tuesday night from ________ in the States.
2. Elizabeth Parnell also hoped Peter to add ________ — the revised budgets for discussion at the meeting.
3. Elizabeth Parnell wants ________ can phone her today.

IV. Role-play.

You work for "First Travel" travel agency in New York. A customer will call you to book a flight. Take his or her reservation. Ask questions about information of the name, date, destination etc. (Only China Airlines is available at these times at \$679 one way or \$989 round trip).

3. Discussing Business Issues

(Telephone Conversations 46 - 50)

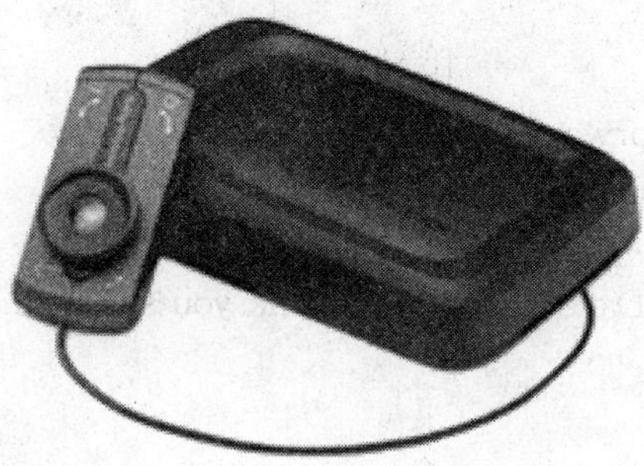

Telephone Conversation 46

New Words and Expressions

promote *v.* 促进,推进;提升
lobby *n.* 门厅,大厅;休息室
banquet *n.* 宴会,盛宴
look forward to 盼望

Caller 1: Hello.
Caller 2: Hello. Can I speak to Stan Summers, please?

Caller 1: Speaking.
Caller 2: Oh. Mr. Summer. You don't know me, but this is Carl Mattews. I'm calling on behalf of Dave Kennedy.

Caller 1: Oh. So you're a friend of Dave's. How is he anyway?
Caller 2: Oh, he's doing well and will be promoted again.

Caller 1: That's good to hear. Carl, what are you doing in New York?
Caller 2: Dave and I are attending a conference[1] at the Hilton until Thursday. And Dave is busy now. So he gave me your telephone number and let me give you a call. He wants to know if you will have any time at all to get together[2] tonight or Thursday evening.

Caller 1：Well，tonight there's a banquet I have to go to. But Thursday evening I'm free.
Caller 2：Good. Thursday evening. And what time would suit you best?

Caller 1：Seven-thirty would be good for me.
Caller 2：Yes，that's fine. So that's 7:30 p. m. on Thursday at Hilton. I'll book the table[3]. And my room is 2120. Dave's is 2122. You can call us from the lobby and I'll come down.

Caller 1：Fine. I'm looking forward to it!
Caller 2：Me，too. See you on Thursday，then.

Caller 1：Please say hello to Dave for me and thank you so much for calling me. Good-bye.
Caller 2：Good-bye.

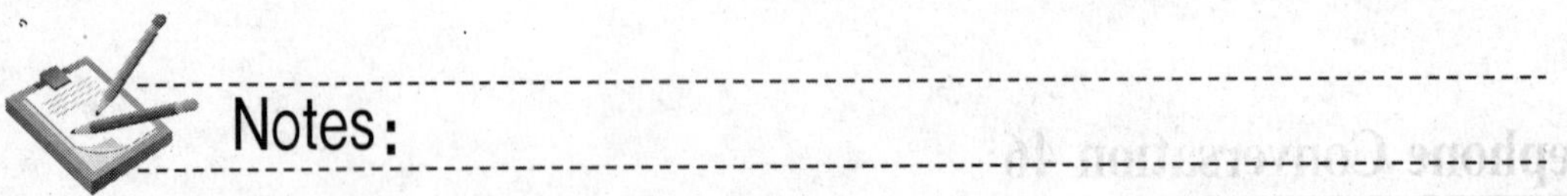

Notes:

1. attend a conference：参加会议。
2. get together：聚会。
3. book the table：预订座位。

Exercise A：Answer the following questions.

1. Who is calling Stan Summers?
2. What is Dave doing until Thursday?
3. What does Dave want to know?
4. When will Carl Mattews be free?
5. What time is suitable for Stan Summers?
6. What is Dave's room number?

Exercise B：Listen to the conversation and fill in the blanks.

1. Can I ________ Stan Summers，please?
2. I'm calling ________ Dave Kennedy.
3. So he gave me your telephone number and let me ________.
4. And what time would ________?
5. You can ______ from the lobby and I'll come down.
6. Please ________ Dave for me and thank you so much for calling me.

Exercise C：

Here is Stan Summers' schedule. Please fill in the blank with the missing information according to the conversation.

	Mon. 2011-07-18	Tue. 2011-07-19	Wed. 2011-07-20	Thur. 2011-07-21	Fri. 2011-07-22
morning	9:00 meet Tom steward, production Manager	10:00 Attend the board meeting	8:00 a business trip to New York		9:15 attend a sales conference
afternoon	12:00 Lunch with Mr. Peter Silver, sales manager			2:45 telephone meeting with David Noble, Director of Marketing at Saimbury's Bank	2:00 golf with Mr. Mark Link
evening		20:00 Attend a banquet in Central Garden Hotel		?	

Telephone Conversation 47

New Words and Expressions

relocation *n.* 搬迁；重新安置
similar *a.* 相似的
visa *n.* 签证
work permit 工作许可
transport *n.* 运输，交通
major *a.* 主要的
handle *v.* 处理

Caller 1：Amanda Ramose speaking.
Caller 2：Hi，Amanda. It's Bob here.

Caller 1：Hi，Bob. Did you get my report about ERS[1]?
Caller 2：Yeah，about the relocation. Now you said you were contacting another company?

Caller 1：Yeah，I spoke to one this morning. It's called Worldwide Relocation. And they look good.
Caller 2：And how well do they meet our needs? Do they stand up to ERS[2]?

Caller 1：In fact，they are quite similar. Like ERS，they have a house search service.
Caller 2：And do they handle all the paperwork? Visas，work permits . . . ?

Caller 1：Yeah. No problems there.
Caller 2：OK，fine. Now what about transport? You know，removal，shipping.

Caller 1：Let me just . . . Oh right. Here it is. No，this is something they don't offer.
Caller 2：Whereas ERS do. Mmm. How do you feel about that，Amanda?

Caller 1：I don't know，but I don't see this as a major problem. I think it's something you can handle by yourself.

Caller 2：OK. And what else? How about finding schools?

Caller 1：Yeah. They have a school search service. And another interesting thing is that they run orientation and cultural integration programmes[3].
Caller 2：Sounds interesting，Amanda. So what's your feeling on this?

Caller 1：Well，neither company meets all our key needs，but there's no one else in the picture[4].
Caller 2：And in terms of cost?

Caller 1：In terms of cost，ERS are offering the best deal. However，cost isn't a major issue here.
Caller 2：You know，it worries me that ERS offers no partner employment assistance[5]. How about worldwide?

Caller 1：Yes，and very successful. The guy I spoke to said that they can normally arrange employment for the partner within three months. And as most of our people have wives or husbands，they do need the service.
Caller 2：Yeah，that's the main problem with ERS. Well，which one do you choose?

Notes:

1. ERS：公司名，全称为 Executive Relocation Services。
2. Do they stand up to ERS? 他们与 ERS 相比怎么样？
3. run orientation and cultural integration programmes：开设适应新环境及文化融合的课程。
4. there's no one else in the picture：没有其他候选的公司。
5. partner employment assistance：合作方就业帮助。

Exercise A: Answer the following questions.

1. Which company offers house search service?
2. Which company can handle paperwork such as visas, work permits?
3. Which company can help with transport?
4. Which company runs orientation and cultural integration programmes?
5. Which company is a better choice in terms of cost?
6. Which company offers partner employment assistance?

Exercise B: Listen to the conversation and fill in the blanks.

1. And how well do they ____________?
2. No, this is something Worldwide don't ________.
3. I don't know, but I don't see this as a ______.
4. Neither company meets all our key needs, but there's on one else ________.
5. However, cost isn't a ________ here.
6. The guy I spoke to said that they can normally arrange employment for the partner ______.

Exercise C: If you are with Amanda, could you help her make a decision which company is a better choice? State your reasons.

Telephone Conversation 48

New Words and Expressions

direct flight 直航
fix up 安排
in transit （飞机、火车）换乘时
option *n.* 选择
confirm *v.* 确认

Caller 1: Mr. Ballito's office.

Caller 2: Good morning. This is the Dongali Airlines Office. Mr. Ballito wanted a seat on the 11 o'clock flight to Sofia next Saturday morning. Is that right?

Caller 1: Yes, that's right. That's the only direct flight that day, isn't it?

Caller 2: Yes, it is. I'm sorry to tell you that it's fully booked[1]. But we do have some seats available for Sunday.

Caller 1：I'm afraid Mr. Ballito has to leave on Saturday. Can't you fix him up with another flight on Saturday[2]?

Caller 2：Well，yes，there is a flight leaving at 2 o'clock on Saturday afternoon，but he would have to change at Athens and wait two hours in transit[3].

Caller 1：Oh，I see. Well，is there any morning flight?

Caller 2：Yes，but it leaves at 5:30 in the morning. Is that OK with you?

Caller 1：It is too early in the morning. Is there any other option?

Caller 2：Sorry，I'm afraid not.

Caller 1：Well，it seems we have to take the afternoon flight.

Caller 2：Fine. Do you want to go economy，business or first class[4]?

Caller 1：Economy class，I think. Mr. Ballito is out of the office at the moment. I'll ask him when he comes in. I'll ring you back this afternoon to confirm the reservation[5].

Caller 2：OK. Our telephone number is 474－7424.

Caller 1：474－7424. Thanks. Good-bye.

Caller 2：Good-bye.

Notes:

1. it's fully booked：票全订完了。
2. Can't you fix him up with another flight on Saturday? 你能不能为他安排另一个周六的航班?
3. but he would have to change at Athens and wait two hours in transit：但他必须在雅典转机，换乘要等候两个小时。
4. go economy，business or first class：乘坐经济舱、商务舱还是头等舱。
5. confirm the reservation：确认订票。

Exercise A：Answer the following questions.

1. Where does Mr. Ballito want to go?
2. Why can't Mr. Ballito take the 11 o'clock flight to Sofia?
3. Is the flight leaving at 2 o'clock on Saturday afternoon a direct flight?
4. Why can't Mr. Ballito take the 5:30 flight?
5. What class will Mr. Ballito take?
6. What flight Mr. Ballito will probably take?

Exercise B: Listen to the conversation and fill in the blanks.

1. Mr. Ballito wanted a seat on the ____________ to Sofia next Saturday morning.
2. Can't you ________ with another flight on Saturday?
3. There is a flight ________ at 2 o'clock on Saturday afternoon.
4. He's out of the office __________.
5. I'll ring you back this afternoon to ____________.
6. Ok. Our telephone number is ________.

Exercise C:

Try to tell your partner the main idea of the conversation. The following sentences might help you.

Mr. Ballito can't get a seat on the eleven o'clock flight because ______________. There is a flight leaving at 5:30 but he can't take it either because ______________. So he may take the 2:00 afternoon flight but he has to ________ and wait ________.

Telephone Conversation 49

New Words and Expressions

concerning *prep.* 关于,就……而论
miss *v.* 错过
get a hold of 找到(某人或某物)
possibility *n.* 可能性
count on 依靠,指望
shuffle *v.* 推掉,推开
feel free to 不要拘束,请随意

Caller 1: Hello, Bill Burton speaking. What can I do for you?
Caller 2: Hello, Mr. Burton. This is Jenny of Bradford and Sons returning your call.

Caller 1: Oh, hi, Jenny. I called you this morning. But you were not in.
Caller 2: I'm sorry you missed me when you called my office this morning. My secretary said you called concerning our meeting next Tuesday?

Caller 1: Yes, Jenny, thank you for returning my call. I'm glad to finally get a hold of you[1]. I wanted to let you know I will not be able to have our meeting next Tuesday. I will be out of town that day. Is there any possibility we can move the meeting to Monday?
Caller 2: I'm sorry, I'm afraid I'm completely booked on Monday. Would it be possible to

postpone until you return?

Caller 1：Oh dear，I was counting on taking care of our meeting before I leave[2]，but I suppose I could shuffle a few things[3]. Yes，we can arrange something. I'll be back Thursday morning. What about Thursday afternoon? Would that work for you[4]?

Caller 2：That should be fine.

Caller 1：Shall we say about 1 o'clock?

Caller 2：1 o'clock might be too early for me. What about 2 o'clock?

Caller 1：Perfect. I'll look forward to seeing you at 2 o'clock next Thursday afternoon.

Caller 2：Me，too.

Caller 1：If you need to change the time，please feel free to call me on my cell phone[5].

Caller 2：Thanks，Mr. Burton. I'll see you on Thursday.

Caller 1：See you. Good-bye.

Caller 2：Good-bye，have a nice trip.

1. I'm glad to finally get a hold of you：很高兴终于找到你。
2. I was counting on taking care of our meeting before I leave：我还指望在我离开前见面呢。
3. I suppose I could shuffle a few things：我想我可以推掉一些事情。
4. Would that work for you? 那样你看行不行?
5. please feel free to call me on my cell phone：请随时打我手机。

Exercise A：Answer the following questions.

1. Was Jenny in the office in the morning?
2. Why is Bill not able to have the meeting next Tuesday?
3. Why Monday is not good for Jenny?
4. When will Bill be back?
5. When will they meet?

Exercise B：Listen to the conversation and fill in the blanks.

1. I'm sorry you ________ me when you called my office this morning.
2. I wanted to ________ I will not be able to have our meeting next Tuesday.
3. Is there any ________ we can move the meeting to Monday?

4. Would it be possible to ________ until you return?
5. If you need to change the time, please ________ me on my cell phone.
6. Goodbye, have a nice ________.

Exercise C: Read the conversation and fill in the form.

From	
To	
Problem(s)	
How to solve it/them?	

Telephone Conversation 50

New Words and Expressions
dentistry *n.* 牙科诊所
remind *v.* 提醒
conflict *n.* 冲突
spot *n.* 地点,场所
time slot 时间窗口

Caller 1: Hello!
Caller 2: Hello, is Doris available?

Caller 1: This is Doris. Who's calling, please?
Caller 2: Hi, Doris, this is Mike calling from Parker's Dentistry. I'm calling to confirm your appointment for tomorrow morning at 9:00 a.m. with Dr. Parker.

Caller 1: Oh, I almost forgot, Thank you for calling to remind me. Actually, I do need to change the time of my appointment. I have a scheduling conflict. And I can't make it[1] that early.
Caller 2: If I put you in at a later spot, would that work out[2]?

Caller 1: It would have to be after lunch. Do you have anything available about 2 o'clock?

Caller 2：Sorry madam，the only opening we have after lunch is 1:15，but I might be able to work you in after 4:00 p. m. Would that be a better time?

Caller 1：That's all right. I think I should be able to make it at 1:15. Can you put me down[3] for that time slot?

Caller 2：No problem. I have your appointment changed from tomorrow morning to tomorrow afternoon at 1:15.

Caller 1：Wonderful. Thanks very much.

Caller 2：You are welcome. Good-bye.

Notes:

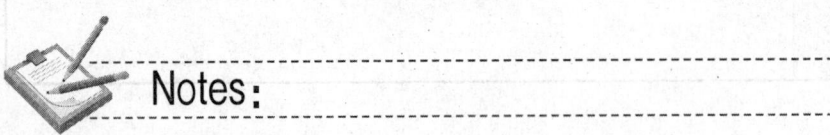

1. make it：做得到，成功。
2. work out：解决。
3. put down：写下，记下。

Exercise A：Answer the following questions.

1. What is Mike calling to say?
2. Why does Doris have to change the time of her appointment?
3. Why can't Doris see the doctor about 2 o'clock?
4. When will Doris see Dr. Parker?

Exercise B：Listen to the conversation and fill in the blanks.

1. I'm calling to __________ for tomorrow morning at 9:00 a. m. with Dr. Parker.
2. I do need to __________ of my appointment. I have a scheduling conflict.
3. I think I should be able to ________ at 1:15 p. m.
4. Can you ________ for that time slot?
5. I have your ________ from tomorrow morning to tomorrow afternoon at 1:15 p. m.
6. ________. Thanks very much.

Exercise C：Translate the following sentences into Chinese.

1. I can't make it that early.
2. If I put you in at a later spot，would that work out?
3. I might be able to work you in after 4.
4. I think I should be able to make it at 1:15 p. m.
5. Can you put me down for that time slot?

Practice

I. Translate the following phrases into Chinese.

1. direct flight
2. get together
3. take a message
4. put down
5. meet with
6. look forward to
7. out of town
8. get a hold of
9. fix ... up
10. on behalf of
11. feel free to
12. in transit

II. Fill in the blank with the phrases in Exercise I.

1. ________ my colleagues, I thank you.
2. We ________ an early reply.
3. Can we ________ tonight?
4. Oh, sorry. Mr. Brown is at a meeting. Can I ________?
5. Mr. Green is not in town. He is ________.
6. I will ________ Peter this evening.
7. AAL ________ 250 is a ________ to New York.
8. I can easily ________ for the night.
9. He is a busy person; I can not even ________ him.
10. Please ________ ask me anything you want ________ know.

III. Listen to the telephone conversation and fill in the blanks.

1. It's ________ since we met last time.
2. How about you? ________.
3. Tim arrived in Dongguan ________, and he wants to hold a ________ with his college classmates.
4. Some others will ________ Shenzhen and Guangzhou.
5. Are you ________ on that day?
6. We haven't gathered ________.
7. I'm ________ Friday.

IV. Role-play.

1. You are contacting a regional sales representative in your company. You tell him/her your local contact information so they know who you are and how to get a hold of you.
2. You are Tim. You'd like to book a flight ticket to Hong Kong from Kenney Airport in New York on Thurday 22nd.
3. You are Paula, a new secretary. You receive a call from Rachel Havel to confirm the appointment with your boss tomorrow afternoon.

4. Establishing Business Relations

(Telephone Conversations 51 - 55)

Telephone Conversation 51

New Words and Expressions

exhibition *n.* 展览会
impress *v.* 给……留下印象
exhibits *n.* 展品
on display 在陈列中，在展览中
particularly *adv.* 尤其，特别
design *n.* & *v.* 设计
in great demand 需求很大
coincide with （意见）一致，协调

Caller 1：Hello，Hangzhou Textiles Import and Export Corporation. Sales Department. Zhang Wei speaking.

Caller 2：Hello. Mr. Zhang. This is Jules Brown from Australia. I have been to the exhibition and I must say I have been much impressed by your products，such as silks，woolen knitwear，cotton piece goods，and garments[1].

Caller 1：Thank you for your saying so. On display are most of our products. Have you found anything you are particularly interested in?

Caller 2：Yes，I am interested in your silk blouses.

Caller 1：Our silks are known for[2] their good quality. They are one of our traditional exports. Silk blouses are brightly coloured and beautifully designed.

Caller 2：Oh，yes. I had a look yesterday. I found some of the exhibits fine in quality and beautiful in design.

Caller 1：Some of them are of the latest style[3]. They've met with great favour overseas and are always in great demand.

Caller 2：Really? You know，I travel a lot every year. This is the first time I have been to China. I am really impressed by the country and your friendly people.

Caller 1：I am glad to hear that. Now I've a feeling that we can do a lot of trade in this line[4].

Caller 2：Yes，I think so. I've gone over the catalogue and the pamphlets[5] of your products and I have got some ideas of your exports. We wish to establish relations[6] with you.

Caller 1：Your desire coincides with ours. I think we should meet sometime and have a further discussion about it.

Caller 2：Great. I wonder if I can visit your company to collect more information about your products tomorrow morning.

Caller 1：You are most welcome.

Caller 2：Then I'll be there around 9:00 o'clock. My phone number is 0412 345 678.

Caller 1：0-4-1-2-3-4-5-6-7-8. I am looking forward to seeing you. Mr. Jules Brown. Bye.

Caller 2：Thank you. Mr. Zhang. Bye.

Notes:

1. silks，woolen knitwear，cotton piece goods，and garments：丝绸织品，毛织品，棉织品和衣物。
2. are known for：因……而著名。
3. of the latest style：最新的款式。
4. in this line：在这个行业。
5. the catalogue and the pamphlets：(产品)目录和小册子。
6. establish relations：建立业务关系。

Exercise A：Answer the following questions.

1. What impressed Jules Brown in the exhibition?
2. What is Jules Brown particularly interested in?
3. How are the sales of silk products in overseas market?
4. Is this the first time for Jules Brown to travel in China?

5. When will they meet?
6. What will they discuss about?

Exercise B: Listen to the conversation and fill in the blanks.

1. I have been to the exhibition and I must say I ________ your products.
2. Have you found anything you are ____________?
3. Silk blouses are ________ and ________.
4. I found some of the exhibits fine ________ and beautiful in design.
5. They've met with great favour overseas and are always ____________.
6. We wish to ________ with you.
7. Your desire ________ ours.
8. I think we should meet sometime and have a ________ about it.

Exercise C:

Zhang Wei received a letter after the exhibition from Jules Brown's company. Some of the words are missing. Try to complete the letter according to the information in the conversation.

Dear Sir/Madam,

We are writing to you in the hope of establishing ________ with you.

We have been importers of dress, cotton and silk products for many years. At present, we are interested in various kinds of ________ and should appreciate your catalogues and quotations.

If your price are in line, we believe important business can materialize.

We are looking forward to your early reply.

Yours faithfully,

...

Telephone Conversation 52

New Words and Expressions

trade fair 交易会

square metres 平方米

stand *n.* 展台

expensive *a.* 价高的,贵的

a bit 一点

disappointing *a.* 令人失望的

offer *v.* 提供

Caller 1：Hello，yes，I'm phoning from Altrex. Could I book a space for next June's trade fair?
Caller 2：Certainly. The units are ten，twenty-eight or forty square metres.

Caller 1：Well，our stand is fifteen square metres ...
Caller 2：So you need twenty-eight. There're plenty that size in Hall Dor one left in A.

Caller 1：How much would that one be?
Caller 2：Six hundred and forty five pounds. Units in D are four hundred and eighty.

Caller 1：Make it the one in Hall A — the more expensive one! How many people are you expecting? I heard this year was a bit disappointing?
Caller 2：Yes，it was — but we did have six thousand[1]. Next year we're planning for seven and a half thousand.

Caller 1：Good. Now，we also need a conference room.
Caller 2：Fine，I could offer you the Gresham Room ...

Caller 1：Can you spell the name?
Caller 2：G-R-E-S-H-A-M. There's also the Ferris Room，that's larger. It holds four hundred[2].

Caller 1：How many seats are there in the Gresham Room?
Caller 2：It takes two hundred and fifty.

Caller 1：That's plenty. Can we have the room from ten or ten-thirty?
Caller 2：Let's make it half past ten[3]. Would a 12 o'clock finish be OK?[4]

Caller 1：Perfect.
Caller 2：Now，the room reference number is IMO 5734 and the whole booking is on TF 62880. Use that if you contact us.

Notes:

1. but we did have six thousand：但的确有 6,000 人来参加。助动词 did 起强调作用。
2. It holds four hundred：它能容纳 400 人。
3. Let's make it half past ten：那就 10:30 吧。Half past ten 系回应上句中的 ten-thirty。
4. Would a 12 o'clock finish be OK? 12 点结束行不行？

Exercise A: Answer the following questions.

1. What is Caller 1 calling for?
2. Which is more expensive, Hall D or Hall A?
3. How many people will attend the trade fair?
4. How many people do they expect next year?
5. How many people can the Ferris Room hold?
6. How many people can the Gresham Room hold?

Exercise B: Listen to the conversation and fill in the blanks.

1. Could I ________ for next June's trade fair?
2. Make it the one in Hall A — ______________!
3. Now, we also need ___________.
4. ______________ are there in the Gresham Room?
5. Now, the room reference number is ________ and the whole booking is on ________.
6. Use that if you ________ us.

Exercise C: Altrex. booked a space for next June's trade fair. Choose the right answer.

Unit	A. twenty-eight	B. Forty
Hall	A. Hall D	B. Hall A
Conference room	A. Gresham	B. Ferris
Time	A. 10:00 - 12:00	B. 10:30 - 12:00

Telephone Conversation 53

New Words and Expressions

tent *n.* 帐篷
clothing range 各类服装
large quantities 大批量
pound *n.* 英镑
(be, get) in touch 与……联系

Caller 1: Good morning. Adventure Holidays Equipment. Philip Sykes speaking.

Caller 2: Good morning, Mr. Sykes, it's Julie Ventnor from Polareach Ltd. I spoke to you briefly last week and you sent us your brochure.

Caller 1: That's right. Was it useful?

Caller 2: Well, we're not really interested in the tents and other equipment, but we may want to order from your clothing range.

Caller 1: Oh right. Have you got one of our order forms[1]?
Caller 2: Yes, but first I need some information on the payment terms[2]. These are quite important because, as I think I said last time, we're interested in purchasing quite large quantities.

Caller 1: Right. What sort of quantities are you thinking of?
Caller 2: We'll want about two thousand pounds worth of goods[3] for each of our ten stores, so we'll probably be giving you orders of around twenty thousand pounds a month.

Caller 1: I'm very pleased to hear that. Can I send the information to you later today?
Caller 2: That'll be fine. Thanks.

Caller 1: If the terms are acceptable, may I suggest a meeting towards the end of January?
Caller 2: Yes, that would be good. Let me see. I can do the 23rd or the 30th.

Caller 1: The 23rd is no good for me, I'm afraid.
Caller 2: Let's say January the 30th then. I'll be in touch at a later date to confirm the time[4].

Caller 1: OK, that's fine. Bye.
Caller 2: Bye.

1. order forms：订单(表格)。
2. payment terms：付款条约。
3. about two thousand pounds worth of goods：大约价值 2 000 英镑的货物。
4. I'll be in touch at a later date to confirm the time：过几天我会与你联系确定时间。

Exercise A: Answer the following questions.

1. What does Julie want to order?
2. Has she got the order forms?
3. What quantities will she purchase every month?
4. Will they meet towards the end of January?
5. Which date is good for Philip?

Exercise B: Listen to the conversation and fill in the blanks.

1. I spoke to you briefly last week and you ________________.
2. we're not really interested in ______________, but we may want to order from your ________.

3. we'll probably be giving you orders of around ______________.
4. If the terms are acceptable, may I suggest a meeting ______________?
5. The 23rd's ________ for me, I'm afraid.
6. I'll be in touch at a later date to ______________.

Exercise C: True or False. Correct the false statements.

1. This is the first time Julie has contacted Philip Sykes from Adventure Holidays equipment Ltd.
2. Julie Ventnor are interested in buying the tents and other equipment.
3. Julie Ventnor is asking for more information about payment terms.
4. Julie Ventor will probably be giving orders of around twenty thousand pounds a month.
5. Philip will meet Julie again on the 23rd of January.

Telephone Conversation 54

New Words and Expressions

catering *n.* 供应伙食,承办酒席
reception *n.* 招待会
launch *v.* 发起,开始
campaign *n.* 活动,运动
Head Office 总部
boardroom *n.* (董事会)会议室
similar *adj.* 类似的

Caller 1: Hello, Executive Catering Services, Anna speaking. How can I help you?
Caller 2: Hello Anna, this is Julian Russell from Family Holidays. We met at the Christmas party held in Anna Hotel last year[1].

Caller 1: Yes, I remember you. How is everything going[2]?
Caller 2: Fine. I wondered if you could do some catering for us next week. We're having a small reception — it's to launch a new advertising campaign. Would you be free?

Caller 1: When exactly is it, Mr. Russell?
Caller 2: Next Thursday — that's May the second.

Caller 1: Oh yes, I can do that. Where will you be holding it?

Caller 2: We thought we'd have it at Head Office and use the Boardroom because there's enough room for everyone there.

Caller 1: OK. What sort of things would you like?

Caller 2: Just a light lunch, I think, so that people can eat while they move around and talk to each other. You did something similar for us last year — we'd be happy to have the same menu again.

Caller 1: Right, I'll look in my diary and see what you had. Oh, I nearly forgot to ask you, how many should I cater for?

Caller 2: Well, I think most people will be able to come. Perhaps around 25. No, let's say 30 to be sure.

Caller 1: Right. Thank you for getting in touch, Mr. Russell, I'll send you confirmation of the arrangements by the end of the week.

Caller 2: Thank you. I really appreciate it[3]. Bye.

Caller 1: Bye.

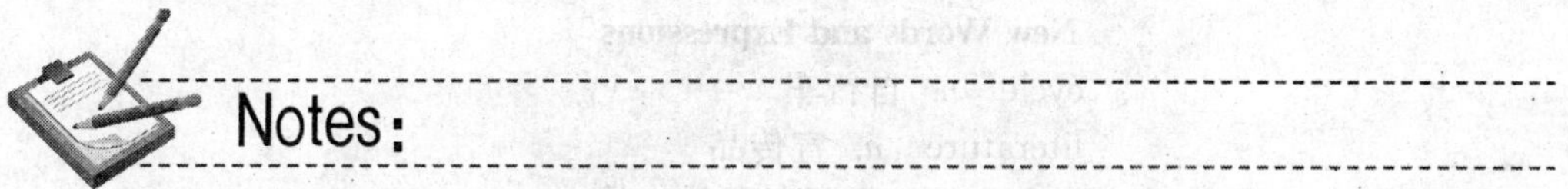

1. the Christmas party held in Anna Hotel last year：去年在安娜宾馆举办的圣诞晚会。
2. How is everything going? 最近怎么样?
3. I really appreciate it：我非常感谢。

Exercise A: Answer the following questions.

1. Where did they meet for the first time?
2. What is Julian calling for?
3. When will they have the reception?
4. Will they use the Boardroom?
5. What food should be prepared?
6. How many people will be there?

Exercise B: Listen to the conversation and fill in the blanks.

1. How is everything ________?
2. I wondered if you could ________ for us next week.
3. We're having a small reception — it's to launch ________.
4. Just a light lunch, I think, so that people can eat while they ________ and talk to

each other.

5. I'll send you ______________________ by the end of the week.
6. Thank you. I really ________ it.

Exercise C: Read the conversation and fill in the form.

From	
time	
place	
food	
Number of people	

Telephone Conversation 55

New Words and Expressions

cycle *n.* 自行车
literature *n.* 宣传品
racing wear 赛车穿戴物品
pull-out leaflet 折页广告
specifications *n.* 规格
(be) short of 缺，缺少
spare parts 配件
demonstration *n.* 演示

Caller 1：Whiteway Cycles. Phil Moore，Sales.
Caller 2：Hello，Phil. It is me-Sandra.

Caller 1：Hi，Sandra. What can I do for you?
Caller 2：We've just got the sales literature for the Paris trade show next week，and there are some problems. Can you get it sorted out for me[1]?

Caller 1：Go ahead[2].
Caller 2：First of all，we need some more catalogues for racing wear. There's a lot of interest in it，especially the shorts and shoes.

Caller 1: OK. Er, thirty enough?

Caller 2: That should do it. And you know the little pull-out leaflet for the children's cycles? Well, there's a mistake on the third page. The specifications for the wheels are wrong.

Caller 1: Oh, that's bad. We'll change that and get you new copies by the weekend. Anything else?

Caller 2: Erm ... yes, the touring cycles — the lightweight ones — I can't find any price lists for them. Please ask if they've been sent out.

Caller 1: OK. And are you all right for order forms[3]?

Caller 2: No! Thanks for reminding me. We're short of forms for spare parts. Could you send us some more?

Caller 1: Right, got that[4].

Caller 2: Oh, can you give Steve McCormack a ring[5] and remind him of the product demonstration[6] next week?

Caller 1: Sure.

Caller 2: Thanks, Phil. That's it then. Bye.

Notes:

1. Can you get it sorted out for me? 你能帮我解决吗?
2. Go ahead: 说吧。
3. And are you all right for order forms? 订单(表格)够不够?
4. Right, got that: 行,知道了。
5. give sb a ring: 给……打电话。
6. product demonstration: 产品演示。

Exercise A: Answer the following questions.

1. Why is Sandra calling?
2. What catalogues does she need?
3. What is wrong on the third page in the leaflet?
4. Is she short of order forms?
5. Whom will Phil call ?
6. What will Phil remind him of?

Exercise B: Listen to the conversation and fill in the blanks.

1. We've just got the sales literature ________ next week.

2. There's a lot of interest in it, especially ________.
3. Well, there's ________ on the third page.
4. Erm ... yes, the touring cycles —________— I can't find any price lists for them.
5. We're short of forms for spare parts. Could you ____________.
6. Can you give Steve McCormack ________ and remind him of the product demonstration next week?

Exercise C: List the problems that they have.

1.
2.
3.
4.

Practice

I. Translate the following phrases into Chinese.

1. on display
2. in great demand
3. be in touch
4. sort out
5. give sb a ring
6. be known for
7. a bit
8. cater for
9. remind sb of sth
10. be short of

II. Fill in the blank with the phrases in Exercise I.

1. Our school ________ foreign teachers.
2. The price is ________ high. Can you cut it down?
3. China ____________ its large population.
4. Silk products are ________________.
5. The boy ________ the foreign stamps he had collected.
6. We ________ weddings and parties.
7. Our products will be ________ in the exhibition.
8. Thank you for ________.
9. Why not ________ him ________ and explain the whole thing?
10. Please ________ me ________ the meeting at 4 o'clock.

III. Listen to the telephone conversation and fill in the blanks.

1. I've just had ________________ with a man from Electrolin.
2. But I'm ________ from tomorrow, so could you do it for me?
3. For the time being, he's only ________ a customer database.

4. Who's the ________ person? Is it the sales manager?
5. It's the new ________________, Steve McCormack.
6. Can you ________ it before I get back?
7. Should I ________ him immediately?
8. I wouldn't say it's top priority. ________ medium, I'd say.
9. ________ with him when you've got time.
10. I'll ________ you again soon.

IV. Role-play.

1. Mr. Ham is visiting Lily's company to collect more information of its products. He asks to establish business relations with Lily's company.
2. At a trade fair, Mr. Anderson, a foreign trader, notices the advertisement of Mr. Wang's company. The next day he calls to ask for more information.
3. You are from Contact Training. One day, you receive a call from the City Council to ask whether you have someone who could help them with databases and provide a one-week course.

5. Seeking Information about Products & Services

(Telephone Conversations 56 - 60)

Telephone Conversation 56

New Words and Expressions

leather bag 皮手提包
reputation *n.* 名气,名声,名誉
workmanship *n.* 手艺,工艺品,作品
in particular 特别(是)
attractive *a.* 吸引人的
distinguishing *a.* 特有的,有区别的
feature *n.* 特点
chic *a.* 时尚的
brand name 商标名;品牌名
loyalty *n.* 忠诚,忠心
judgment *n.* 判断
inclination *n.* 倾向,意愿
(be) convinced (感到)信服

Caller 1: Hello.
Caller 2: Hello. Can I speak to Yang Lan, please?

Caller 1: Speaking. Who is that speaking?
Caller 2: Hello. Mr. Yang. This is Helen Marsden from Bombay[1] Trade Company. I'm very interested in your leather bags, and would like to know more about them.

Caller 1: Good. Our leather bags have enjoyed a high reputation in the European market[2] because of their fashionable styles, fine workmanship and quality material[3]. Ms. Marsden, what in particular are you interested in?
Caller 2: Well, I find Article No. 311 in your brochure rather attractive.

Caller 1: It's our latest design. Its most distinguishing feature is its chic style[4]. It sells very well.
Caller 2: Mr. Yang, compared with the various well-known brands from Italy and France, what gives your bags a competitive edge[5], in your opinion?

Caller 1: I would say prices. Our bags have the same high quality, but they are more price-competitive[6], thanks to the low labor and raw material costs[7].
Caller 2: That's true. But in terms of[8] rather personal items such as leather bags, brand names still matter a lot, and Italian and French products are still enjoying high customer loyalty[9]. How can you make customers buy yours?

Caller 1: I think customers can make their own judgment, despite their inclination to Italian and French brands. I believe once we have managed our way into these markets[10], these customers will be convinced.
Caller 2: It sounds convincing. Thanks for your introduction, and I know more about your products now. Can you send me a catalogue with your latest price list?

Caller 1: No problem. Can I have your fax number?
Caller 2: My fax number is 46395569.

Caller 1: 46395569. OK, I will fax it to you as soon as possible.
Caller 2: Thank you. I will call you again after receiving the catalogue.

Caller 1: OK. I hope we have a chance to cooperate. Good-bye.
Caller 2: Good-bye.

Notes:

1. Bombay：孟买(印度中西部城市)。
2. enjoyed a high reputation in the European market：在欧洲市场享有极高声誉。

3. fashionable styles，fine workmanship and quality material：时髦的风格，精湛的工艺和高品质的材料。
4. Its most distinguishing feature is its chic style：它最为显著的特点是它的时尚的风格。
5. competitive edge：竞争优势。
6. price-competitive：在价格上有竞争力。
7. thanks to the low labor and raw material costs：由于低廉的劳动力和原材料价格。
8. in terms of：在……方面。
9. enjoying high customer loyalty：享有很高的客户忠诚度。
10. once we have managed our way into these markets：一旦我们设法进入这些市场。

Exercise A：Answer the following questions.

1. Which company is Helen Marsden from?
2. What product are they talking about?
3. Which product is Helen Marsden especially interested in?
4. What is the most distinguishing feature of No. 311?
5. What is the advantage of Mr. Yang's bags?
6. What is Helen Marsden's fax number?

Exercise B：Listen to the conversation and fill in the blanks.

1. Our leather bags have enjoyed a high ________ in the European market.
2. I find Article No. 311 in your brochure rather ________.
3. Italian and French products are still enjoying high customer ________.
4. Can you send me a ________ with your latest price list?
5. Can I have your ________?
6. I will fax it to you ________.

Exercise C：Discuss the following topic with your partner.

Which is more important to you when shopping，quality or brand name? why?

Telephone Conversation 57

New Words and Expressions

aerobic instrument　有氧器械
new version　新款
commercial　*a.* 商业的
superiority　*n.* 优越性，优等

handlebar grip 车把
safety foot straps 安全脚扣
LCD 液晶显示(= Liquid Crystal Display)
meter *n.* 仪表
weigh *v.* 称重
collapsible *a.* 可折叠的
adjustable *a.* 可调整的

Caller 1：Good morning，Young and Fit，Lewis Taylor speaking. Can I help you?
Caller 2：Hi，Lewis，this is Fiona.

Caller 1：Hi，Fiona.
Caller 2：I have read your new catalogue and I'd like to know more about your aerobic instruments.

Caller 1：What in particular are you interested in?
Caller 2：Type No. AC3 and Type No. AC4.

Caller 1：These two items are the new versions of our aerobic cycles. AC3 is popular with sports centers and suitable for commercial use，while AC4 is designed for family use.
Caller 2：What's their superiority?

Caller 1：They have outstanding features：modern design，comfortable padded handlebar grips，safety foot straps and so on. Each of them comes with a LCD meter[1] to measure speed and distance.
Caller 2：That's impressive. Nowadays，all households prefer to keep one or two aerobic instruments at home，so I think AC4 seems more suitable to our market.

Caller 1：That's true. AC4 is much lighter and smaller. It weighs only eleven kilograms，so it's easy to pick up and carry about[2]. And it's only 40 cm wide and 68 cm long，but it has the same high stability as all our other cycles[3]. It's collapsible. When not in use，it folds up for easy storage[4]. I believe it will be a strong selling point in your market[5].
Caller 2：It sounds great. Is the seat adjustable?

Caller 1：Of course，the seat is height-adjustable[6] to make AC4 suitable for every family member.
Caller 2：Good，but isn't the price marked in your catalogue much higher than that of competing products[7]?

Caller 1：Considering its many advantages，I should say[8] the price is fairly reasonable. During the trial sale period[9], we got lots of orders from both overseas and home market. We can assure you that you'll find very good prospects in our products[10].

Caller 2：OK. Thank you very much for your introduction. I'll be there for a trial order tomorrow morning. Is 10 a. m. suitable for you?

Caller 1：10 a. m. is OK. I will be waiting for you. See you then.

Caller 2：See you.

Notes:

1. Each of them comes with a LCD meter：每个都装有液晶显示仪表。
2. easy to pick up and carry about：便于携带。
3. has the same high stability as all our other cycles：具有与其他产品相同的稳定性。
4. When not in use, it folds up for easy storage：不用时可折叠起来方便存放。
5. a strong selling point：有力的卖点。
6. height-adjustable：高度可调节。
7. competing products：竞争产品。、
8. Considering its many advantages, I should say ...：考虑到它所具有的许多优越性，我得说……
9. trial sale period：试销阶段。
10. you'll find very good prospects in our products：你会发现我们的产品具有非常好的前景。

Exercise A：Answer the following questions.

1. What product is Fiona interested in?
2. What is the difference between AC3 and AC4?
3. Which model is more suitable for Fiona's market?
4. How wide is AC4?
5. How long is AC4?
6. What is the selling point of AC4?

Exercise B：Listen to the conversation and fill in the blanks.

1. AC3 is popular with sports centers and suitable for ________________ use, while AC4 is designed for ________ use.
2. AC4 is much ________ and ________.
3. Is the seat ________?
4. I should say the price is fairly ________.
5. We can assure you that you'll find very good ________ in our products.
6. I'll be there for a ________ order tomorrow morning.

Exercise C: Fill in the form to complete the information about AC4.

Weight	Width	Length	Height	Selling point

Telephone Conversation 58

New Words and Expressions

filing cabinet 文件柜
dimension *n.* 尺寸,大小
drawer *n.* 抽屉
finish *n.* 最后一层涂饰

Caller 1: Good morning, Office Design. How can I help you?
Caller 2: Hello. I want to buy a filing cabinet that will fit under my desk[1].

Caller 1: I see. And how high is your desk?
Caller 2: It's 74 centimeters.

Caller 1: That's very good. We've got two filing cabinets, the FC12W and the FC12M, which are both 74 centimeters high.
Caller 2: How big is the FC12W?

Caller 1: I'm sorry?
Caller 2: What are the dimensions?

Caller 1: Well, as I said, it's 74 centimeters high, 50 centimeters wide, and 65 centimeters deep.
Caller 2: That's 74 by 50 by 65. I see. And what about the FC12M?

Caller 1: It's the same size. The difference is that the FC12W is made of wood, and the FC12M is made of metal. W for wood, and M for Metal.
Caller 2: How many drawers have these cabinets got?

Caller 1: They've got two drawers.
Caller 2: I see. And how much do they cost?

Caller 1：The wooden cabinet costs $140. The metal one is cheaper at $90.
Caller 2：And what colors do they come in[2]?

Caller 1：The FC12W comes in red wood finish[3], the FC12M in blue, black and grey paint.
Caller 2：I see. I can't decide now, but I will call you back later after consideration.

Caller 1：No problem. Thank you for calling. Good-bye.
Caller 2：Good-bye.

Notes:

1. a filing cabinet that will fit under my desk：能安放在我的办公桌下面的文件柜。
2. And what colors do they come in? 它们是什么颜色的?
3. in red wood finish：红色木漆。

Exercise A：Answer the following questions.

1. What are the dimensions of FC12W?
2. What is FC12W made of ?
3. What is FC12M made of ?
4. How many drawers have these cabinets got?
5. How much do they cost?
6. What color are they?

Exercise B：Listen to the conversation and fill in the blanks.

1. How ________ is your desk?
2. How ________ is the FC12W?
3. What ________ do they come in?
4. The FC12W comes in ________ wood finish, the FC12M in ____________, ____________ and ________ paint.
5. I can't ________ now.
6. I will call you back later after ________.

Exercise C：Fill in the following form.

Size	Height：________ cm Width：________ cm Depth：________ cm

continued

Number of drawers	
Price	FC12W: $ ______ FC12M: $ ______
Colours	FC12W: ______ wood finish FC12M: blue, ______ or grey metal

Telephone Conversation 59

New Words and Expressions

package *n.* 一揽子计划,整套(服务)
Internet connection 网络连接
unlimited *a.* 无限的,无限制的
broadband *n.* 宽带
special offer 特价
euro *n.* 欧元
website *n.* 网站

Caller 1: Good morning. Business Services Department, Dana speaking.
Caller 2: Hello, I'd like some information about the small business packages[1] you have.
Caller 1: Certainly, Sir. Which services are you interested in?
Caller 2: Well, I need mobiles for my staff of six and an Internet connection for the office, basically.
Caller 1: We have a special offer at the moment for small businesses. It gives you unlimited national calls on both mobiles and landlines[2], a 24-hour broadband connection[3], and no charge for connecting calls.
Caller 2: And how many mobiles does that cover?
Caller 1: The service covers up to ten mobile phone lines.
Caller 2: Can I have more than one computer connected?
Caller 1: The broadband connection is to your computer network or to a single computer. It doesn't matter which you have.
Caller 2: OK, that's good. And how much does this package cost?

Caller 1：The monthly charge is 75 euros for the first three months，on special offer，and then 120 euros after that.
Caller 2：Right. And how long does the contract last?

Caller 1：There is a penalty charge[4] if you cancel the contract before two years.
Caller 2：Well，I want to think about this.

Caller 1：Certainly，Sir. And don't forget that you can find all of these details on our website.
Caller 2：Yes，good idea. OK，thanks very much.

Caller 1：Thank you for calling. Good-bye.
Caller 2：Good-bye.

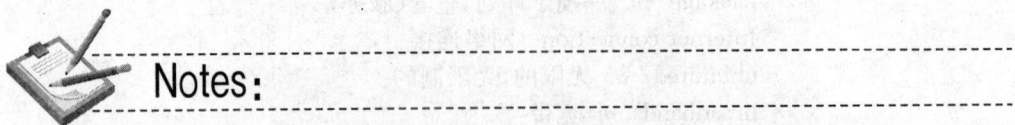

1. the small business packages：为小企业提供的打包服务。
2. unlimited national calls on both mobiles and landlines：无限数量的国内移动电话和座机电话。
3. a 24-hour broadband connection：24 小时宽带连接。
4. penalty charge：罚款。

Exercise A：Answer the following questions.

1. What information is the client asking about?
2. How many mobiles does the service cover?
3. How much does this package cost?
4. How long does the contract last?
5. What will happen if the client cancels the contract before two years?
6. Where can the client find all the details about the service?

Exercise B：Listen to the conversation and fill in the blanks.

1. I need mobiles for my staff of ________.
2. We have a special offer at the moment for small ________.
3. The broadband connection is to your computer network or to a ________ computer.
4. The monthly charge is 75 euros for the first three months，on ________，and then 120 euros after that.
5. It doesn't ________ which you have.
6. There is a ________ charge if you cancel the contract before two years.

Exercise C：You are going to find out information about your classmates' experiences with Internet service providers (ISP).

Questions	Person 1	Person 2	Person 3	Person 4
Name of ISP				
Broadband connection				
Technical support				
Monthly-charge				
Overall opinion				

Telephone Conversation 60

New Words and Expressions

telephone banking　电话银行
account　*n.* 账户
day-to-day　*a.* 每天的，日常的
PIN　个人识别码(Personal Identification Number)；密码
check balance　查询余额
pay bills　支付账单
order a statement　要求提供结算(单)
transfer money　转账
normal　*a.* 正常的
automated　*a.* 自动的

Caller 1：Good morning. Customer Services Department. Can I help you?
Caller 2：Yes, I'd like some information on your telephone banking service.

Caller 1：Certainly. Do you have an account with us?
Caller 2：Yes, I do.

Caller 1：Well, with our telephone banking service you can do all your day-to-day banking over the telephone at any time of day or night[1].
Caller 2：How does it work?

Caller 1：All you do is ring up, key in your PIN number[2], choose the service you want and then just follow the instructions. It's as easy as that.

Caller 2：And what can I actually do over the phone?

Caller 1：You can check your balance，pay bills，order a statement or transfer money. All your normal day-to-day banking.

Caller 2：Does it cost anything?

Caller 1：No. The number is a free phone number，so you don't pay for your calls and the service is part of your normal bank account.

Caller 2：Oh right. And can I phone at any time of the day?

Caller 1：Yes，you can. There's an automated answering machine[3] and staff are available 24 hours-a-day，seven days a week[4].

Caller 2：It sounds good. Thanks for your information.

Caller 1：You're welcome.

Caller 2：Good-bye.

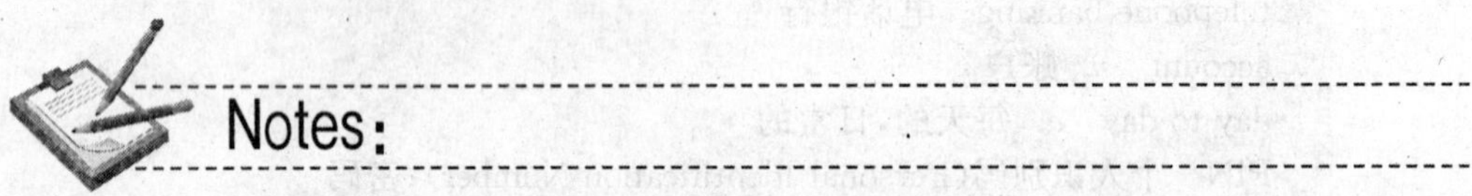

1. you can do all your day-to-day banking over the telephone at any time of day or night：无论白天黑夜什么时候，你都可以通过电话做你的日常银行业务。
2. key in your PIN number：键入你的密码。
3. automated answering machine：自动答录机。
4. staff are available 24 hours-a-day，seven days a week：每天 24 小时，每周 7 天都有员工候着。

Exercise A：Answering the following questions.

1. What services does the telephone banking offer?
2. What are the steps of using the service?
3. Do you need to key in your PIN number if you use the service?
4. What can customers do with the service?
5. Is the service free?
6. When can you use the telephone banking service?

Exercise B：Listen to the conversation and fill in the blanks.

1. Good morning. ________ department.
2. Do you have an ________ with us?

3. How does it ________?
4. The number is a ________ number.
5. There's an ________ answering machine.
6. Staff are available 24 hours-a-day, ________ days a week.

Exercise C: Fill in the form to complete the information about telephone banking.

Process	
Service available	
Cost	
Service time	

Practice

I. Translate the following phrases in to Chinese.

1. brand name
2. customer loyalty
3. price list
4. as soon as possible
5. selling point
6. trial sale
7. special offer
8. telephone banking
9. check balance
10. pay bills
11. transfer money
12. bank account

II. Fill in the blank with the phrases in Exercise I.

1. During the ________ period, we got lots of orders from both overseas and home market.
2. I will fax it to you ________.
3. Can you send me a catalogue with your latest ________?
4. Italian and French products are still enjoying high ________.
5. It will be a strong ________ in your market.
6. ________ still matter a lot.
7. The service is part of your normal ________.
8. With our ________ service you can do all your day-to-day banking over the telephone.
9. You can ________, ________, or ________.
10. We have a ________ at the moment for small businesses.

III. Listen to the conversation and fill in the blanks.

1. Can I ________ with you about the e-commerce website?
2. There's still ________ for a software engineer, though.
3. ... do you think you could produce a report for ________ by the end of the week?
4. ... would you make sure you ______ the objectives in clear, straightforward language?

IV. Role-play.

1. A customer calls you to ask about your products. Introduce the products to the customer.
2. A customer calls you to ask about your service. Introduce the service to the customer.

6. Seeking Information about Prices & Contracts

(Telephone Conversations 61 – 65)

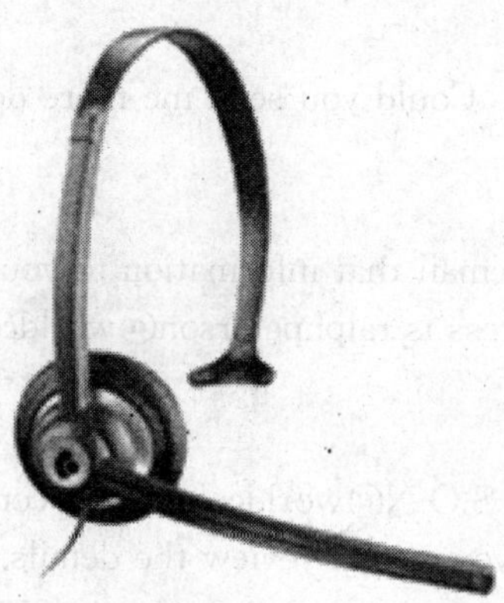

Telephone Conversation 61

New Words and Expressions
promotional *a.* 促销的
sound card 声卡
quantity *n.* 数量
terrific *a.* 好极的

Caller 1: Hello. Sales Department. This is Betty Fields speaking.
Caller 2: Hello, Ms Fields. This is Ralph Peterson at World Computers.

Caller 1: Yes, how may I help you?
Caller 2: I'm interested in a couple of items in your new catalog, and I would like to know the prices.

Caller 1: Great. We're offering a special promotional price[1] on a few of the items.
Caller 2: Really? Great!

Caller 1: Which items did you have in mind?
Caller 2: We're particularly interested in your new RS – 5 sound card shown on page five of your catalog. I would also like more details about the model RS – 4 card on page seven.

Caller 1：OK. The price on the RS－5 is forty-five U. S. dollars for quantities up to five hundred units[2]. Then we offer quantity discounts for larger orders[3].

Caller 2：And the price on the RS－4?

Caller 1：The RS－4 is one of our promotional items this month. For orders received by the end of the month，the price is thirty-three dollars each. That price is good on any size order[4].

Caller 2：That price sounds good. Could you send me more details about the RS－4，including the specifications?

Caller 1：Certainly. I can fax or email that information to you this afternoon.

Caller 2：Terrific. My email address is ralphpeterson@worldcomputers. com. That is R-A-L-P-H-P-E-T-E-R-S-O-N.

Caller 1：R-A-L-P-H-P-E-T-E-R-S-O-N@worldcomputers. com. Is that right?

Caller 2：Right. I'll get back to you after I review the details. Thank you. Good-bye.

Caller 1：Thanks for calling. Good-bye.

Notes:

1. a special promotional price：促销特价。
2. The price on the RS－5 is forty-five U. S. dollars for quantities up to five hundred units：RS－5 的价格为每个 45 美元，凡购买 500 个以下均为此价。
3. We offer quantity discounts for larger orders：对于更大的订单，我们给予数量折扣。
4. That price is good on any size order：任何数量的订单都是这个价格。

Exercise A：Answer the following questions.

1. Why does Ralph Peterson make the call?
2. What kind of product are they talking about?
3. What is the price of RS-five?
4. What is the price of RS-four?
5. What is the email address of Ralph Peterson?
6. When will Betty Fields send the information?

Exercise B：Listen to the conversation and fill in the blanks.

1. Hello. ________ Department. This is Betty Fields speaking.
2. The RS－4 is one of our ________ items this month.

3. That price is good on any size ________.
4. Could you send me more details about the RS-4, including the ________?
5. I can ________ or ________ that information to you this afternoon.
6. I'll ________ you after I review the details.

Exercise C: Role-play.

You want to order a large quantity of memories, so you make a call to ask about the price information from the potential supplier. Make a telephone dialogue with your partner.

Telephone Conversation 62

New Words and Expressions

Alibaba 阿里巴巴(电子商务公司)
sample *n.* 样本,样品
sensor tap 感应龙头
fax *n.* 传真
v. 发传真

Caller 1: Good morning. Yocoss Computers, Sally speaking. Can I help you?
Caller 2: Yes, I'm Alan French. I find your company in Alibaba, and I want to buy one sample of the sensor tap. Who can I talk to?

Caller 1: I'll put you through to Mr. Brian Fraser in Sales Department. Just a moment, please.
Caller 2: Thank you.

Caller 3: Good morning, Brian speaking. What can I do for you?
Caller 2: My name is Alan French. I find your company in Alibaba, and I want to buy one sample of the sensor tap.

Caller 3: Which model are you interested in?
Caller 2: I'd like to know the price of the model C7251B.

Caller 3: The price of C7251B is $100.
Caller 2: And how about the model C7253A?

Caller 3: The price of C7253A is $98. I can send you some details of these two models to you.

May I have your fax number?

Caller 2：Yes，of course. My fax number is double six-three-five-double eight-one-five.

Caller 3：Double six-three-five-double eight-one-five.

Caller 2：Right. I will contact you after receiving your fax. Thank you.

Caller 3：Thank you for calling. Good-bye.

Caller 4：Good-bye.

Exercise A：Answer the following questions.

1. How does Alan French get to know Yocoss Computers?
2. Why does Alan French make the call?
3. Who is Alan French talking to?
4. What is the price of C7251B?
5. What is the price of C7253A?
6. What is Alan French's fax number?

Exercise B：Listen to the conversation and fill in the blanks.

1. I'll ________ you ________ to Mr. Brian Fraser in sales department.
2. Which ________ are you interested in?
3. I'd like to know the ________ of the model C7251B.
4. I can send you some details of these two ________ to you.
5. May I have your ________?
6. I will ________ you after receiving your fax.

Exercise C：Discuss the following topic with your partner.

What factors will you consider when choosing a supplier? Why?

Telephone Conversation 63

New Words and Expressions

portable electric heater 手提式电暖气

place an order 下订单

rating *n.* 等级，评级

exception *n.* 例外

durable *a.* 耐用的，持久的

blade *n.* 叶片，刀锋

rotate *v.* 旋转
initial *a.* 开始的
in line with 与……一致

Caller 1: Hello.
Caller 2: Hello. Is Bryan Ross available?

Caller 1: Yes, speaking. Who is that?
Caller 2: I'm David Hoffman. I'm very interested in your portable electric heater. But I'd like more information before placing an order.

Caller 1: I'd be happy to answer your questions.
Caller 2: There's one problem I think I ought to mention. How about the energy efficiency rating[1] of the heater?

Caller 1: As you know, heaters tend to be high energy users[2]. Our model E22 is no exception. But although this heater is not as energy-efficient[3] as some, it does have the most durable, problem-free electric motor of any heater we've tested[4].
Caller 2: That sounds impressive. Do you have any similar, but smaller, heaters?

Caller 1: Yes, our model E25 only has a four-inch blade, but it's made to rotate at high speeds.
Caller 2: What are the prices on these models?

Caller 1: The large model goes for $58, and the smaller unit is $39.
Caller 2: Are those prices the lowest you can offer? I don't know if those prices will work for us[5].

Caller 1: We might be able to offer you a 10% cut on your initial order[6]. 10% off is about as low as we can go[7].
Caller 2: That sounds more in line with what we can handle[8]. Well, let me check my figures and get back to you on it.

Caller 1: OK, Mr. Hoffman. If you have any other questions, just give me a call.
Caller 2: Thank you very much, Mr. Ross. Good-bye.

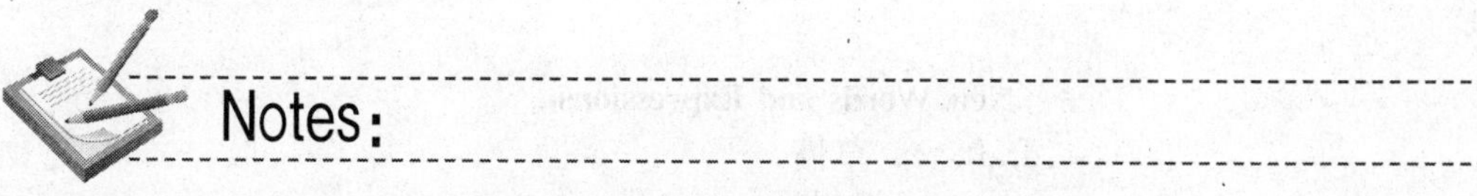

1. energy efficiency rating: 能源效率等级。

2. high energy users：高能耗产品。
3. energy-efficient：节能的。
4. it does have the most durable，problem-free electric motor of any heater we've tested：在我们检测过的电动马达中，它是最耐用、最少故障的。
5. I don't know if those prices will work for us：我不知道这些价格我们能否接受。
6. on your initial order：首次订单。
7. 10% off is about as low as we can go：我们最多也只能降10%。
8. That sounds more in line with what we can handle：这听上去和我们能接受的较为接近。

Exercise A：Answer the following questions.

1. Why does David Hoffman make the call?
2. How is the energy efficiency rating of E22?
3. What are the advantages of E22?
4. What are the advantages of E25?
5. What are the prices of E22 and E25?
6. What is the lowest price Bryan Ross can offer?

Exercise B：Listen to the conversation and fill in the blanks.

1. Is Bryan Ross ________?
2. I would like more information before placing an ________.
3. Do you have any similar，but ________，heaters?
4. We might be able to offer you a 10% cut on your ________ order.
5. 10% off is about as ________ as we can go.
6. That sounds more in line with what we can ________.

Exercise C：Fill in the form about E22 and E25.

	Price	Features
E22		
E25		

Telephone Conversation 64

New Words and Expressions

draft *n.* 草稿
v. 起草

clarify *v.* 澄清，阐明
deadline *n.* 最后期限
shipment *n.* 装运
effect *v.* 执行

Caller 1: Hello, Henry Wallace speaking. What can I do for you?

Caller 2: Hello, Mr. Wallace. This is Sophie from Vitesse Sportwear returning your call. I'm sorry you missed me when you called my office this morning.

Caller 1: Yes, I called you about our contract. I've seen your draft for our contract. I wonder whether you can clarify shipment in more detail.

Caller 2: What's your suggestion?

Caller 1: I'd like you to put in a deadline for both the shipment.

Caller 2: We have agreed that the second shipment would occur no later than 30 days after the first shipment.

Caller 1: You're right. But we need to specify the date for the first shipment.

Caller 2: OK. How about October 18th, 2012?

Caller 1: That is acceptable.

Caller 2: So now I'll change the terms regarding shipment as follows, "The first shipment to be made on or before October 18th, 2012 and the second shipment to be effected within 30 days after the first shipment."

Caller 1: That sounds good. Though we have established the deadline for both the first shipment and the second shipment, I'd prefer that you ship as soon as possible.

Caller 2: Of course.

Caller 1: Thank you very much.

Caller 2: If you have any other suggestion, please contact me.

Caller 1: Good. I give you a call after sending you the new draft contract.

Caller 2: OK. Good-bye.

Exercise A: Answer the following questions.

1. When did Henry call Sophie?
2. Why did Henry call Sophie?
3. What does Henry Wallace want to do with the draft contract?

4. What's the deadline for the first shipment?
5. When will the second shipment occur?
6. Does Sophie agree to revise the contract?

Exercise B: Listen to the conversation and fill in the blanks.

1. This is Sophie from Vitesse Sportwear ________ your call.
2. I'm sorry you ________ me when you called my office this morning.
3. I called you about our ________.
4. I'd like you to put in a ________ for both the shipment.
5. We need to specify the ________ for the first shipment.
6. If you have any other ________, please contact me.

Exercise C: Discuss the following topic with your partner.

What principles should we stick to when drafting a contract?

Telephone Conversation 65

New Words and Expressions

bring up　提出
stipulate　*v.* 规定
pack　*v.* 捆扎，打包
machine parts　机器零件
truck base　汽车底座
revise　*v.* 修改

Caller 1: Hello!
Caller 2: Hello, is Juliet available?

Caller 1: This is Juliet. Who's calling, please?
Caller 2: Hi, Juliet, this is John calling from Fastmotor. I'm calling to talk about our draft contract.

Caller 1: Any questions?
Caller 2: I made a very close study of the draft last night. There is a point which I'd like to bring up.

Caller 1: What is it?

Caller 2: The packing. It's stipulated in the contract that all the machine parts should be packed in wooden cases. This can be done with the machine parts, but it's impossible to pack a truck base like that.

Caller 1: I see. We agree to a different packing for the truck.
Caller 2: This can easily be done.

Caller 1: Is there anything else?
Caller 2: There is nothing more. Thank you very much.

Caller 1: When should we sign the contract?
Caller 2: We'll revise the contract this evening, and have it ready to be signed tomorrow morning at ten. How's that?

Caller 1: Perfect. See you tomorrow then.
Caller 2: See you.

Exercise A: Answer the following questions.

1. Why does John call?
2. How will the machine parts be packed?
3. What's John's requirement for packing?
4. Does Juliet accept John's suggestion?
5. Will they change the contract?
6. When will they sign the contract?

Exercise B: Listen to the conversation and fill in the blanks.

1. I'm calling to talk about our ________ contract.
2. There is a ________ which I'd like to bring up.
3. It's ________ to pack a truck base like that.
4. We ________ a different packing for the truck.
5. When should ________ the contract?
6. We'll ________ the contract this evening.

Exercise C: Role-play.

You have a suggestion about the draft contract, so you call your business partner to discuss about it.

Practice

I. Translate the following phrases in to Chinese.

1. place an order
2. in line with

3. establish the deadline
4. bring up
5. agree to
6. put through
7. energy-efficient
8. get back to
9. a couple of
10. sign the contract

II. Fill in the blank with the phrases in Exercise I.

1. I'll ________ you after I review the details.
2. When should we ________?
3. This heater is not as ________ as some.
4. That sounds more ________ what we can handle.
5. I'd like more information before ________.
6. There is a point which I'd like to ________.
7. We ________ a different packing for the truck.
8. We have ________ for both the shipment.
9. I'm interested in ________ items in your new catalogue.
10. I'll ________ you ________ to Mr. Brian Fraser in sales department.

III. Listen and fill in the blanks.

1. It's about the ________ for constructing the factory in Melbourne.
2. We specified that we couldn't complete in ________.
3. ... we'll be awarded the contract for their next project if we can ________.

IV. Role-play.

1. You are the purchasing manager of a company and you want to order some office supplies for your staff. Now, you make a call to one of your suppliers and ask for relative information.
2. You have read the draft contract and you want to add some more details about delivery date. Now, you make a call to your business partner.

7. Negotiating with Clients

(Telephone Conversations 66 - 70)

Telephone Conversation 66

New Words and Expressions

superior *a.* 高级的，较高的
make a profit 赚钱
meet each other half way 各让一半
rock bottom 最低点

Caller 1：Hello.
Caller 2：Hello. Can I speak to Mark Jenkins，please?

Caller 1：Speaking.
Caller 2：It's Henry from H & G. We've studied your offer carefully.

Caller 1：What do you think of it?
Caller 2：We're surprised to find that your price is 25% higher compared with other companies.

Caller 1：But you fully know that our product is of superior quality[1]. Other products can't be compared with it.
Caller 2：True. But it's also a fact that your price is too high.

Caller 1：Then what's your idea of a good price?
Caller 2：I would say 20% off the listed price.

Caller 1：Impossible. We won't make any profit at that price. 10% off is the best we can do.
Caller 2：It's still too high.

Caller 1：Our quality is far beyond comparison[2]. Besides，the market is advancing[3]. Our goods can always find a good sale.
Caller 2：Other companies are also saying that their products are the best.

Caller 1：Let's meet each other half way[4]. I'll drop anther 5%. That's definitely my rock bottom price[5].
Caller 2：All right. 15% off. That's settled.

Caller 1：Let me check the figures，and then get back to you. Good-bye.
Caller 2：Good-bye.

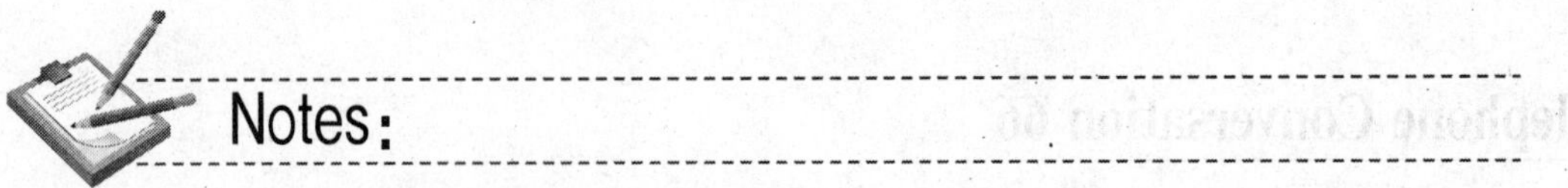

1. of superior quality：质量上乘。
2. far beyond comparison：无法比拟。
3. the market is advancing：市场价格在提升。
4. Let's meet each other half way：各退一步。
5. That's definitely my rock bottom price：这绝对是最低价了。

Exercise A：Answer the following questions.

1. Which company is Henry working in?
2. Why does Henry make the call?
3. Why is Henry surprised?
4. How does Mark think of their products?
5. Why don't Mark agree 20% off?
6. What do they agree to finally?

Exercise B：Listen to the conversation and fill in the blanks.

1. We've studied your ________ carefully.
2. You fully know that our product is of ________ quality.
3. I would say ________ off the listed price.
4. Our quality is far ________ comparison.

5. The market is ________.
6. Let me check the ________, and then get back to you.

Exercise C: Discuss the following topic with your partner.

What should you consider when negotiating prices with your business partner?

Telephone Conversation 67

New Words and Expressions

individually *ad.* 个别地，单独地
carton *n.* 纸板箱
window display 橱窗展示
fragile *a.* 易碎的
reinforce *v.* 增强，加固
dampness *n.* 潮气
waterproof *a.* 防水的
complaint *n.* 抱怨，投诉
precaution *n.* 预防，防备

Caller 1: Hello, Carmen Selleys speaking.
Caller 2: Hi, Carmen, it's Suzanne again. I want to discuss the packing with you.

Caller 1: Sure. We usually pack our shirts individually in plastic bags, ten dozen to one carton[1].
Caller 2: Acceptable. But please pay attention to the design of the inner packing. All the packages must be ready for window display.

Caller 1: Please don't worry. All the bags are beautifully designed to come in line with local market preference at your end[2].
Caller 2: All right. You mentioned cartons, didn't you? I'm afraid cartons are not strong enough.

Caller 1: But we're only talking about shirts. They're not fragile goods. Besides, cartons are light and easy to handle.
Caller 2: Well, I just mean they're easily breakable.

Caller 1: There's no need to worry. We can reinforce the cartons with straps[3].
Caller 2: Look, these goods will have to go a long way before they arrive at our port. What if

dampness gets into the packages?

Caller 1：All the cartons are lined with plastic sheets[4]，so they're absolutely waterproof. I can assure you.

Caller 2：As I just said，it's a long-distance transportation. I really don't want to take any risks.

Caller 1：You need have no fears about that. Our way of packing has been widely accepted by other clients，and we have received no complaints whatsoever so far.

Caller 2：Really? Then I suppose there is no other choice.

Caller 1：Don't worry，Suzanne. Packing is our concern too[5]，so we'll take every possible precaution to ensure[6] that our products reach our customers in every corner of the world.

Caller 2：I hope so. Good-bye.

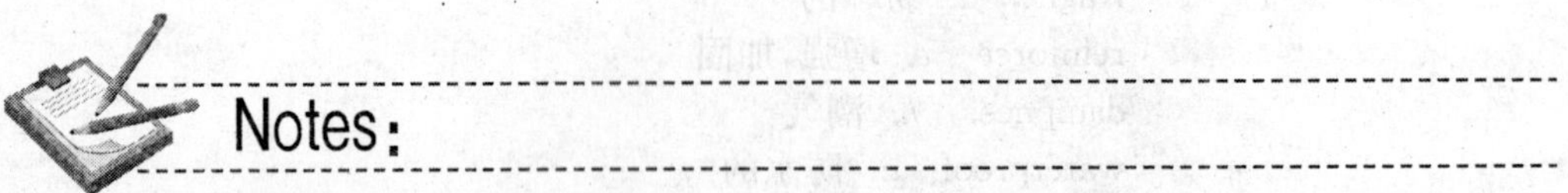

Notes:

1. ten dozen to one carton：10 打装一箱。
2. All the bags are beautifully designed to come in line with local market preference at your end：所有包装袋设计精美，为贵方市场所喜爱。
3. reinforce the cartons with straps：用包装带加固纸箱。
4. lined with plastic sheets：四周用塑料纸包装。
5. Packing is our concern too：包装也是我们所关心的。
6. we'll take every possible precaution to ensure ...：我们会采取一切预防措施，以保证……

Exercise A：Answer the following questions.

1. Why does Suzanne make the call?
2. What is Suzanne worrying about?
3. What kind of bags will the shirts be packed in?
4. What does Carmen assure Suzanne?
5. Will Carmen change the packing?
6. What do other clients think of Carmen's packing?

Exercise B：Listen to the conversation and fill in the blanks.

1. We usually pack our shirts individually in plastic bags，________ to one carton.
2. All the packages must be ready for ________.
3. All the bags are beautifully designed to come in line with local market ________ at your end.

4. Cartons are ________ and ________ to handle.
5. It's a ________ transportation.
6. I really don't want to take any ________.

Exercise C: Fill in the form to complete the information about packing.

Packing	Features
Inner packing	
Cartons	

Telephone Conversation 68

New Words and Expressions

inspection *n.* (质量)检查
commodity *n.* 商品
partially *ad.* 部分地;局部地
ready goods 现货;成品
freight *n.* 运费

Caller 1: I'd like to talk to Mr. Tony Lin, please.
Caller 2: Yes, speaking. Who's calling, please?

Caller 1: How are you, Tony? This is Brown.
Caller 2: Fine, thank you. Mr. Brown, is there anything I can help you?

Caller 1: I want to know if you have shipped the goods of our order No. 215 as scheduled[1].
Caller 2: We are sorry to tell you that this shipment will be delayed to the end of this month because the production loss is high. Besides, we need to do inspection to ensure the quality.

Caller 1: Then when is the earliest shipment we can expect?
Caller 2: By the middle of October, I think.

Caller 1: It's too late. You see, October is the season for this commodity in our market.
Caller 2: I understand.

Caller 1: But we need this shipment urgently. Can you partially ship some ready goods to us?

Caller 2：How much quantity do you need urgently?

Caller 1：Can you air 2,000 pieces to us tomorrow? And the rest is to be shipped before the end of this month.

Caller 2：OK. I'll arrange to ship 2,000 pieces by air tomorrow with freight prepaid[2], as it's our fault to cause the delay.

Caller 1：Thank you for your help. Good-bye.

Caller 2：Good-bye.

Notes:

1. as scheduled：按计划。
2. with freight prepaid：预付运费。

Exercise A：Answer the following questions.

1. Why does Brown call?
2. Have the goods been shipped as scheduled?
3. Why has the shipment been delayed?
4. When will Tony ship the 2,000 pieces?
5. Who will pay the freight?
6. When will the rest goods be shipped?

Exercise B：Listen to the conversation and fill in the blanks.

1. I want to know if you have shipped the goods of our order ________ as scheduled.
2. Besides, we need to do 100% ________ to ensure the quality.
3. October is the ________ for this commodity in our market.
4. How much ________ do you need urgently?
5. Can you air ________ pieces to us tomorrow?
6. It's our ________ to cause the delay.

Exercise C：Fill in the form about the telephone conversation.

Problem	
Reason	
Solution	

Telephone Conversation 69

New Words and Expressions

insurance coverage 订单保险额
invoice value 发表金额
comply with 服从，遵守
excessive *a.* 太多了
quotation *n.* 报价
insurance agent 保险代理

Caller 1：I'd like to talk to Mr. William Goren，please.
Caller 2：Yes，speaking. Who's calling，please?

Caller 1：Hi，William. This is Robin.
Caller 2：Hi，Robin. Is there anything I can help you?

Caller 1：I'm calling to discuss the level of insurance coverage you've requested for your order[1].
Caller 2：I believe that we have requested an amount twenty-five percent above the invoice value[2]. Right?

Caller 1：Yes，that's right. We have no problem in complying with your request，but we think that the amount is a bit excessive.
Caller 2：We've had a lot of trouble in the past with damaged goods.

Caller 1：I can understand your concern. However，the normal coverage for goods of this type is to insure them for the total invoice amount plus ten percent[3].
Caller 2：We would feel more comfortable with the additional protection.

Caller 1：Unfortunately，if you want to increase the coverage，we will have to charge you extra for the additional cost[4].
Caller 2：But the insurance was supposed to be included in the quotation.

Caller 1：Yes，but we quoted you normal coverage at regular rates[5].
Caller 2：I see.

Caller 1：We can，however，arrange the extra coverage[6]. But I suggest you contact your insurance agent there and compare rates.

Caller 2：You're right. It might be cheaper on this end.

Caller 1：Fax me whatever rates you find there and I'll compare them with what we can offer.
Caller 2：OK. I'll call you back. Good-bye.

Notes:

1. I'm calling to discuss the level of insurance coverage you've requested for your order：我想和你讨论一下你方订单要求的保险金额。
2. We have requested an amount twenty-five percent above the invoice value：我方要求保险金额是发票金额的25％。
3. the normal coverage for goods of this type is to insure them for the total invoice amount plus ten percent：这种货物的正常保费是发票金额的10％。
4. if you want to increase the coverage，we will have to charge you extra for the additional cost：如果你想提高保险金额，我们将为增加的成本向你方收取额外的费用。
5. We quoted you normal coverage at regular rates：我方报的是正常保险费率下的保险金额。
6. arrange the extra coverage：增加额外的保险金额。

Exercise A：Answer the following questions.

1. Why does Robin call?
2. What is the normal coverage for the goods?
3. How much has William required for insurance?
4. How does Robin think of William's requirement for insurance?
5. What does Robin suggest?
6. Does William accept Robin's suggestion?

Exercise B：Listen to the conversation and fill in the blanks.

1. We have requested an amount ________ percent above the invoice value.
2. We think that the amount is a bit ________.
3. We've had a lot of trouble in the past with ________ goods.
4. We would feel more comfortable with the ________ protection.
5. The insurance was supposed to be included in the ________.
6. I suggest you contact your ________ agent there and compare rates.

Exercise C：Role-play.

In the above telephone conversation，William accepts Robin's suggestion to consult an insurance agent，so he makes the call. Make a telephone dialogue about it with your partner.

Telephone Conversation 70

New Words and Expressions

weight *n.* 重量
evidence *n.* 证据
consignment *n.* 托运，寄售
supervise *v.* 监督，管理
excessive *a.* 过多的，过分的
moisture *n.* 潮湿，湿气
retained sample 保留的样品

Caller 1：Can I speak to Ma Yun，Please?
Caller 2：Speaking. Who's calling，please?

Caller 1：Hi，Mr. Ma. This is Daniel Black. It's about the 5，000 tons soybeans we bought from you Last February.
Caller 2：What's the problem?

Caller 1：It was found 25 tons short-weight on its arrival. That is to say，there is a difference of 25 tons between the actual landed weight and the invoiced weight[1].
Caller 2：How can that be? Do you have any evidence?

Caller 1：Certainly. I have sent you the inspection certificate[2] from London. Have you received it?
Caller 2：Let me check ... Yeah，I get it.

Caller 1：We therefore claim for compensation for the loss.
Caller 2：Wait a minute. You should be clear enough that the final consignment of our soybeans on loading was taken by actual physical weighing of the product. The scales were checked[3] and the captain of the ship was there to supervise the weighing. He can prove that full weight was delivered.

Caller 1：The problem mainly stems from[4] the excessive moisture of the goods. If there hadn't been the excessive moisture，we wouldn't have called for a settlement[5].
Caller 2：Was your analysis made on the retained samples[6]? We will take no responsibility for moisture on arrival of goods at their destination.

Caller 1：No problem. Our analysis was made on the retained samples.

Caller 2：Well，I'm afraid we'll have to have the retained samples rechecked before we settle it. It's very unfortunate for you anyway and we'll try our best to solve it. But we have to respect the inspection analysis.

Caller 1：All right. It's understood. I'll call you after reporting to my manager.
Caller 2：OK. Good-bye.

Notes：

1. a difference of 25 tons between the actual landed weight and the invoiced weight：发票重量和实际到岸重量之间相差 25 吨。
2. inspection certificate：货检证书
3. The scales were checked：称重量的秤检查过了。
4. stems from：源于……
5. If there hadn't been the excessive moisture，we wouldn't have called for a settlement：如果不是因为大豆含有过多的水分，我们也不会来理赔了。
6. Was your analysis made on the retained samples? 你的分析是基于你方保留的样品吗？（因为样品中的大豆含有很多的水分，所以认定大豆在运输过程中由于水分的丢失，导致到岸后的重量比离岸时轻了 25 吨）

Exercise A：Answer the following questions.

1. Why does Daniel Black call?
2. What is the difference between the actual landed weight and the invoiced weight?
3. Who can prove the full weight of soybeans has been delivered?
4. What my cause the short weight?
5. Was Daniel's analysis made on the retained samples?
6. What will Mr. Ma probably do next?

Exercise B：Listen to the conversation and fill in the blanks.

1. It's about the ________ tons soybeans we bought from you Last February.
2. I have sent you the inspection ________ from London.
3. We therefore claim for ________ for the loss.
4. The problem mainly stems from the excessive ________ of the goods.
5. It's very ________ for you anyway.
6. We have to ________ the inspection analysis.

Exercise C：Role-play.

After rechecking the retained samples，it's proved that Mr. Ma should take responsibility for the short-weight of soybeans. Therefore, Mr. Ma makes a call to Daniel Black to apologize and discuss compensation. Make a telephone conversation about it with your partner.

Practice

I. Translate the following phrases in to Chinese.

1. make a profit
2. rock bottom
3. window display
4. be supposed to
5. comply with
6. stem from
7. on arrival
8. by air
9. production loss
10. take precaution

II. Fill in the blank with the phrases in Exercise I.

1. The problem mainly ________ the excessive moisture of the goods.
2. We will ________ at that price.
3. I'll arrange to ship 2,000 pieces ________ tomorrow with freight prepaid.
4. We will take no responsibility for moisture ________ of goods at their destination.
5. That's definitely my ________ price.
6. All the packages must be ready for ________.
7. This shipment will be delayed to the end of this month because the ________ is high.
8. We'll ________ to ensure that our products reach our customers in every corner of the world.
9. We have no problem in ________ your request.
10. The insurance ________ be included in the quotation.

III. Listen and fill in the blanks.

1. I thought it would be a very ________ to hold the shareholders' meeting you're arranging.
2. ... but I looked at the conference hall and the ________ lounge and either would be perfect ...
3. Anyway, they're both large rooms with ________ ...
4. The number's ________.

IV. Role-play.

1. You will purchase 5 tons of peanuts and make a call to negotiate the price with the supplier.
2. You are worried about the packing of the goods, so you make a call to the business partner.
3. You want to make a call to negotiate the deposit with your supplier.

Unit 3

The Telephone System

1. The Telephone *

Step 1　New Words and Expressions

call log　呼叫日志
call re-direction　呼叫改发
conference-calling　电话会议
convert　*vt.* 转变,变换
document scanning　文件扫描
duration　*n.* 持续时间
electrical impulse　电脉冲
extension　*n.* 电话分机
file　*vt.* 提出申请;提起诉讼
lab　*n.* 实验室
patent　*n.* 专利;专利权
replace　*v.* 代替
simplify　*v.*　简化
Valentine's Day　情人节
voicemail　*n.* 语音邮件

Step 2 Reading

A. Talk about the following pictures in English.

B. Read the passage and do the exercises.

A clever device, the telephone has greatly changed the lives of most people. It is able to change the sound of the human voice into tones[1], and then back again into a tone that sounds like the human voice. Michael Faraday[2] began the process of inventing the telephone in 1831 when he proved that waves could be converted to electrical impulses[3]. Unfortunately, no one used his discovery for another thirty years, until Johann Reiss[4] built a simple model that changed electricity to sound and then back again.

In the United States, Alexander Graham Bell[5] and Elisha Gray[6] were competing to design the first telephone. Both men filed for patents[7] on Valentine's Day[8] 1876, with Bell filing only two hours before Gray filed his. Bell had worked steadily for many years to design his system, while Gray had grown discouraged with his project, after he built the first telephone receiver in 1874.

The first telephone call was made one month later on 6 March 1876 when Bell called for his assistant, Watson, to come into his lab to help him. "Watson, come here quickly, I need you!" Which were the first words spoken by telephone. This conversation proved to be the start of the Bell Telephone Company, which later became the American Telephone and Telegraph Company (AT&T)[9], the largest telephone company in the world.

Notes:

1. change the sound of the human voice into tones：将人说话的声音转化为音频。

2. Michael Faraday：迈克尔·法拉第(1791—1867)英国物理学家、化学家。
3. could be converted to electrical impulses：可被转化为电脉冲。
4. Johann Reiss：约翰·赖斯，德国科学家。
5. Alexander Graham Bell：亚历山大·格雷厄姆·贝尔(1847—1922)，苏格兰人，被认为是电话发明人。
6. Elisha Gray：以利沙·格雷(1835—1901)，美国电气工程师。
7. filed for patents：申请专利。
8. Valentine's Day：情人节(每年2月14日)。
9. the American Telephone and Telegraph Company (AT&T)：美国电话电报公司。

Exercise A: Answer the following questions.

1. What did Johann Reiss invent?
2. When was the first telephone receiver built?
3. What were the first words spoken by telephone?
4. What does AT&T stand for?

Exercise B: Fill in the blanks according to the text.

1. The ____________ has greatly changed the lives of most people.
2. ________ began the process of inventing the telephone in ________.
3. ________________ and Elisha Gray were competing to design the first telephone.
4. The first telephone call was made one month later on ________.

Exercise C: True or false. Correct the false statements.

1. Elisha Gray invented the telephone.
2. Both men filed for patents on Valentine's Day 1876.
3. The first telephone call was made on 6 March 1876.
4. Gray built the first telephone receiver in 1874.

Step 3 Practice

I. Discuss in pairs.

1. Who invented the telephone?
2. Why did he invent it?
3. How does this invention change the world?

II. Talk about the following pictures and guess when they were used.

Step 4 Supplementary Reading

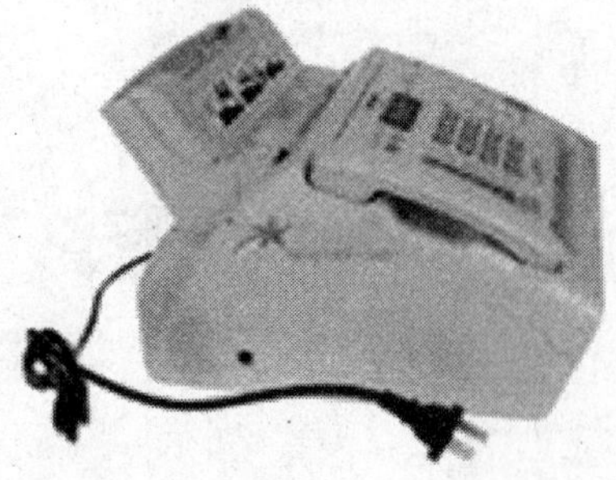

Most business telephone systems offer functions that simplify making and receiving telephone calls.

One of the simplest telephone functions is voicemail, which allows callers to leave messages while you're away from the phone or on another call. Voicemail can be stored, sent to another person and received away from the office. Leaving voicemail on for long periods can upset customers. If you won't be in office for any length of time, consider using call re-direction[1].

When businesses are on different sites, conference calling[2] allows them to work together. It lets you make telephone calls with more than two people — a useful way of managing work on projects involving different teams or businesses[3].

Businesses can use call logging[4] to record the number, timing and duration of calls made from each extension. This function helps ensure your phone system is used in the right way.

You can use it to watch work in departments where phone use is a basic business activity, such as customer service or sales departments.

Sending faxes used to be important, however, this function has been replaced by document scanning[5] and email.

Notes:

1. using call re-direction：使用呼叫改向。
2. conference calling：电话会议。
3. managing work on projects involving different teams or businesses：对涉及不同团队或企业的项目进行管理。
4. call logging：录音监听服务器，可以对通话全程录音。
5. document scanning：文件扫描。

True or false. Correct the false statements.

1. One of the most complex telephone functions is voicemail, which allows callers to leave messages while you're away from the phone or on another call.
2. Conference calling allows you make telephone calls with more than two people.
3. Businesses can use call logging to record the number, timing and duration of calls made from each extension.
4. Sending faxes used to be important, and this function has not been replaced by document scanning and email.

2. Landline Telephones *

Step 1 New Words and Expressions

decade *n.* 十年
cellular *a.* 蜂窝的,蜂窝电话的
dominant *a.* 占优势的,支配的
connectivity *n.* (网络)连接;连线
verbal *a.* 口头的,非书面的
diverse *a.* 不同的,互异的;多种多样的
transmitter *n.* 送话器,话筒
staple *n.* 日常必需品
subscribership *n.* 电话用户
balloon *v.* 激增
desert *v.* 抛弃,遗弃,离弃
statistics *n.* 统计,统计资料
emergence *n.* 出现;浮现
consistent *a.* 始终如一的,前后一致的
fidelity *n.* 忠诚,尽责,精确
operational *a.* 操作的,运作的
outage *n.* (水、电等的)中断
whereas *ad.* 反之;却;而
relay tower 基站塔
immobility *n.* 固定性,静止
redundant *a.* 多余的,过剩的
obsolete *a.* 废弃的,淘汰的;过时的,老式的

Step 2 Reading

A. Talk about the following pictures in English.

B. Read the passage and do the exercises.

What Is a Landline Telephone?

A landline telephone[1] is a device using a physical line for connection to a telecommunications network[2]. Landline phones were developed in the late 19th century and became common around the world in the following decades. Cellular networks[3] in the 2000s began to replace landlines as the dominant form of telephone connectivity.

Rise of the Landline Telephone

The invention of the landline telephone made verbal communication over long distances possible. Early telephone models were diverse in their makeup[4]; some used liquid transmitters[5] while others used carbon transmitters[6]. As technology continued to improve in the field of telecommunication, the landline telephone became cheaper and easier to operate. Since its invention in 1876, the landline telephone has connected billions of people and become a technological staple[7] of societies around the world.

Peak Usage

Landline telephones reached their highest global subscribership numbers[8] early in the 21st century. In the year 2000, there were 16 fixed telephone lines for every 100 people in the world. In 2005 and 2006, the number peaked at 20 fixed-lines for every 100 people. In developed nations, subscribership numbers peaked in the years 2000 and 2001, with 57 fixed-lines per 100 people.

Decreasing Use

Statistics reveal that landline telephone usage has begun to decrease with the growth of wireless technology. In 1995, wireless cell phone subscriptions totaled 33.8 million in the

United States. In 2008, subscriptions ballooned to[9] 270.3 million, increasing by 699 percent over the 13 year period. During this time, 26.6 percent of American homes deserted their landline telephone entirely. Nearly 16 percent of Americans now receive all or almost all of their calls on wireless devices. From 2005 to 2010, landline-only homes[10] dropped from 34.4 percent to 12.9 percent. These statistics reveal that with the emergence of wireless telecommunication technology, landline telephones may become obsolete in upcoming decades[11].

Notes:

1. landline telephone：有线电话，座机。
2. telecommunications network：电信网络。
3. Cellular networks：移动网络。
4. diverse in their makeup：构造多种多样。
5. liquid transmitters：液体送话器。
6. carbon transmitters：碳精送话器。
7. a technological staple：一个主要的技术性的日常必需品。
8. reached their highest global subscribership numbers：全球订户数量达到最高。
9. ballooned to：猛增至……
10. landline-only homes：只拥有座机的家庭。
11. become obsolete in upcoming decades：在未来数十年被淘汰。

Exercise A：Answer the following questions.

1. When were landline phones developed?
2. What happened as technology continued to improve in the field of telecommunication?
3. How many fixed-lines for every 100 people in 2005 and 2006?
4. What was the reason for landline telephone usage decreasing?

Exercise B：Fill in the blanks.

1. A landline telephone is a device with a ____________ to a telecommunications network.
2. Cellular networks in the 2000s began ____________ as the dominant form of telephone connectivity.
3. The invention of the landline telephone made ____________________ possible.
4. In developed nations, ________________ in the years 2000 and 2001.
5. In 1995, ________________ subscriptions totaled 33.8 million in the United States.
6. Nearly 16 percent of Americans now ________________ on wireless devices.
7. From 2005 to 2010, ________________ from 34.4 percent to 12.9 percent.
8. With the emergence of __________________, landline telephones may become obsolete in upcoming decades.

Exercise C: True or false. Correct the false statements.

1. Landline phones became common around the world in the late 19th.
2. In the year 2000, there were 16 fixed telephone lines for every 100 people in America.
3. Landline telephone usage has begun to fall with the growth of wireless technology.
4. From 2005 to 2010, landline-only homes increased from 34. 4 percent to 12. 9 percent.

Step 3 Practice

I. Discuss in pairs.

1. The rise of landline telephones.
2. The decrease of landline telephones.
3. The future of landline telephones.

II. Talk about the following pictures.

Step 4 Supplementary Reading

Advantages and Disadvantages of Landline Telephones

Even with cell-phone use on the rise and landline use declining, landline telephones do present advantages over cell phones. The biggest advantage is consistent fidelity of the telephone signal[1]. Landlines don't suffer from the signal problems[2] cell phones face during bad weather or in remote areas. Landline telephones do not require an electrical connection and are operational during power outages[3]— whereas cell phones rely on relay towers[4] that must be powered to receive or send a signal.

The biggest disadvantage to landline telephones is their immobility. While cell phones can be taken and used almost anywhere, landline phones can be used only in or near the home or office. The landline may represent a redundant service and an added cost[5] for those with a cell phone, though most basic landline service packages[6] cost less than basic cell-phone plans. Landline phones are quickly losing their quality advantage[7] as cell phones' audio signals and reliability improve.

Notes:

1. consistent fidelity of the telephone signal：稳定、精确地电话信号。
2. signal problems：信号故障。
3. power outages：断电。
4. relay towers：继电器塔。
5. represent a redundant service and an added cost：构成重复多余的服务和额外增加的成本。
6. basic landline service packages：基本的座机服务费。
7. quality advantage：质量上的优势。

True or false. Correct the false statements.

1. Landline telephones have little advantages over cell phones.
2. Landlines will have no signal problems during bad weather.
3. Cell phones depend on relay towers to receive or send a signal.
4. The landline may cost more for those with a cell phone.

3. Mobile Phones *

Step 1 New Words and Expressions

whilst *conj.* = while
access *n.* 接近,进入;进入的权利;使用
capability *n.* 能力,才能;性能,功能
cloning *n.* 无性繁殖系化,克隆
commercially *ad.* 商业上
cordless *a.* 不用电线的;无绳的
demonstrate *v.* 论证,证明;演示;说明
geographic *a.* 地理学的;地理的
internal corrosion 内腐蚀
modify *v.* 更改,修改;缓和,减轻
momentary *a.* 暂的;瞬间的
nefarious *a.* 违法的,邪恶的
penetrate *v.* 穿过;透过;渗透入
subscription *n.* 预订;订阅
telephony *n.* 电话制造(或操作)法;电话(通讯方式)
transmit *v.* 传送,传达

Step 2 Reading

A. Talk about the following pictures in English.

B. Read the passage and do the exercises.

Mobile Phone

A mobile phone (also known as a cellular phone, cell phone and a hand phone) is a device that can make and receive telephone calls over a radio link whilst moving around a wide geographic area. It does so by connecting to a cellular network provided by a mobile phone operator, allowing access to[1] the public telephone network. By contrast, a cordless telephone[2] is used only within the short range of a single, private base station.

In addition to telephony, modern mobile phones also support a wide variety of other services such as text messaging[3], MMS[4], email, Internet access, short-range wireless communications, business applications, gaming and photography. Mobile phones that offer these and more general computing capabilities are referred to as smartphones[5].

The first hand-held mobile phone was demonstrated by Dr. Martin Cooper of Motorola in 1973, using a handset weighing around 1kg. In 1983, the Dyna TAC 8000x model was the first to be commercially available[6]. In the twenty years from 1990 to 2011, worldwide mobile phone subscriptions grew from 12.4 million to over 5.6 billion, penetrating the developing economies and reaching the bottom of the economic pyramid[7].

Notes:

1. allowing access to：可以进入。
2. cordless telephone：无绳电话。
3. text messaging：短信。
4. MMS，multimedia messaging service：多媒体短信服务。
5. smartphone：智能手机。

6. commercially available：成为商品。
7. the bottom of the economic pyramid：经济金字塔的底部。

Exercise A：Answer the following questions according to the above text.

1. How does a mobile phone receive telephone calls?
2. What is the disadvantage of a cordless telephone written in the passage?
3. What advantages do mobile phones have besides telephony?
4. What kind of phones can be regarded as smartphones?

Exercise B：Fill in the blanks according to the text.

1. A mobile phone can ____________ over a ____________ whilst moving around a wide geographic area.
2. Modern mobile phones can ____________ such as ____________，email，Internet access，etc.
3. The first hand-held mobile phone was demonstrated by ____________ in 1973.
4. In 1983，the ____________ was the first to ____________.

Step 3 Practice

I. Discuss in pairs.

1. What is the most important function of your mobile phone besides making or receiving calls?
2. In what way can you use your mobile phone to learn English?
3. Supposing without mobiles，what would our world be like?

II. Talk about the following pictures.

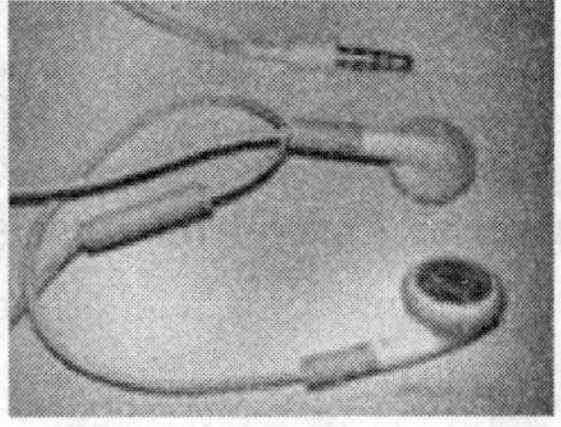

Step 4 Supplementary Reading

Problems with Cell Phones

A cell phone，like any other electronic device，has its problems：

- Generally，non-repairable internal corrosion of parts[1] results if you get the phone wet or use wet hands to push the buttons. Consider a protective case. If the phone does get wet, be sure it is totally dry before you switch it on so you can try to avoid damaging internal parts.

- Extreme heat in a car can damage the battery or the cell-phone electronics. Extreme cold may cause a momentary loss of the screen display[2].
- Analog cell phones[3] suffer from a problem known as "cloning". A phone is "cloned" when someone steals its ID numbers[4] and is able to make fraudulent calls on the owner's account[5].

Here is how cloning occurs: When your phone makes a call, it transmits the ESN and MIN[6] to the network at the beginning of the call. The MIN/ESN pair is a unique tag for your phone — this is how the phone company knows who will be bill for the call. When your phone transmits its MIN/ESN pair, it is possible for nefarious sorts[7] to listen (with a scanner) and capture the pair. With the right equipment, it is fairly easy to modify another phone[8] so that it contains your MIN/ESN pair, which allows the nefarious individual to make calls on your account.

Notes:

1. non-repairable internal corrosion of parts：无法维修的内部腐蚀零件。
2. momentary loss of the screen display：屏幕暂时不能显现；短时间黑屏。
3. Analog cell phones：模拟手机。
4. ID numbers：身份证号。
5. make fraudulent calls on the owner's account：在户主的账户上打电话。
6. ESN，electronic serial number：手机的电子序列号；MIN：是系统内部对每个用户的标识。
7. nefarious sorts：不法分子。
8. modify another phone：修改另一台电话。

True or false. Correct the false statements.

1. If the phone gets wet, better not use it before it is totally dry so as not to damage the internal parts.
2. Extreme cold may cause damage to the battery or the cell-phone electronics.
3. When your phone makes a call, it translates the ESN into your native language to the network.
4. With the right equipment, it is fairly easy to modify another phone so that it can make calls on your account.

4. Internet Telephones *

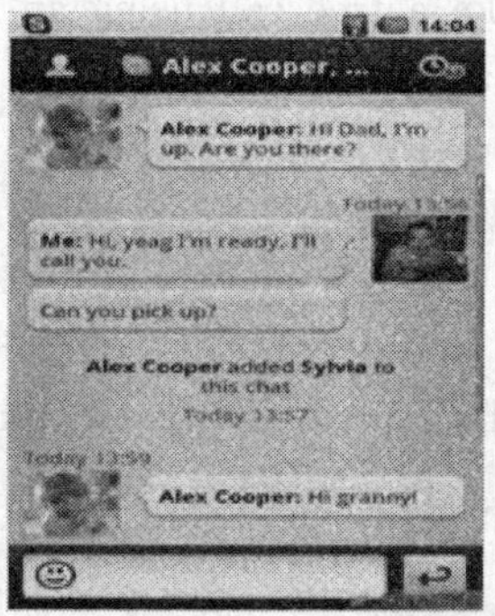

Step 1 New Words and Expressions

destination *n.* 目的地,终点
incredibly *adv.* 难以置信地,很,极为
integration *n.* 整合,完成
length *n.* (距离、尺寸的)长度
Skype 一种简单的免费软件,使您能够在数分钟之内在世界上的任何角落拨打免费电话
via *prep.* 通过,凭借
overlook *v.* 忽略

Step 2 Reading

A. Talk about the following picture in English.

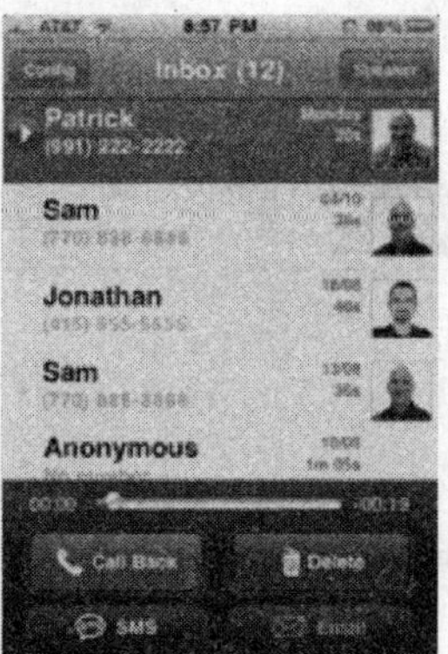

B. Read the passage and do the exercises.

5 Ways to Make Free Internet Phone Calls

You really can make free phone calls using the Internet! Free internet phone programs let you make free phone calls. To make a free call using an Internet phone, you might have to download free phone call software or use a soft phone[1] from an Internet phone provider website.

1. Google Voice

As of September 2011, Google Voice is the very best way to make free Internet phone calls. With Google Voice, you can make free phone calls, free PC to phone calls (via Google Talk browser plug-in[2]), and free PC to PC calls (also via Google Talk).

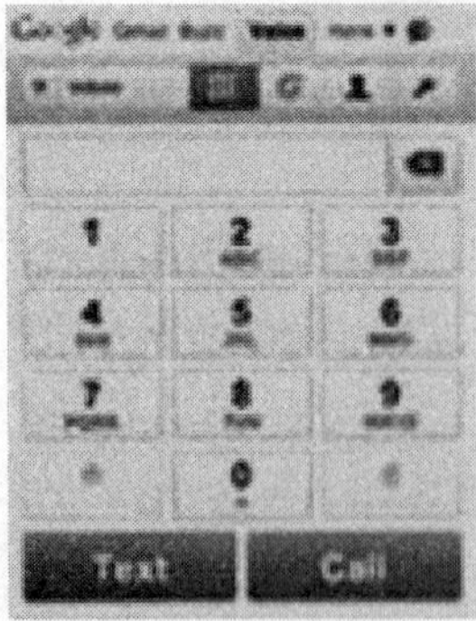

2. iCall

iCall is another tool you can use to make free internet phone calls. With iCall, you can make free calls from PC to phone using their free software.

3. Freebuzzer

Another Internet phone that can be used to make free phone calls is Freebuzzer.

Freebuzzer works a lot like Google Voice in that it connects your phone with the phone number you dial. Your free call is limited to a very short two minutes and you can only make three free calls per day.

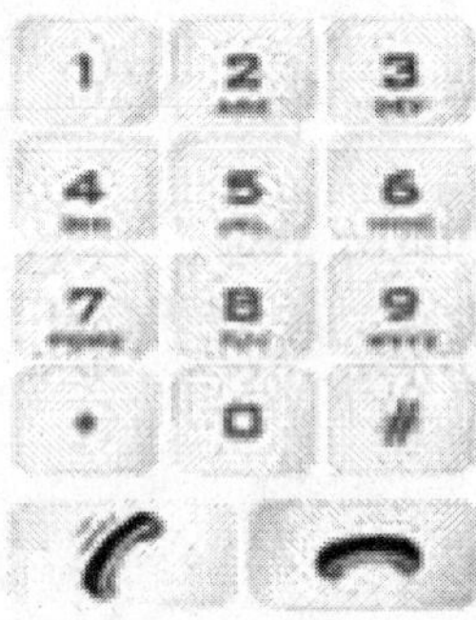

4. EvaPhone

What makes EvaPhone unique is that you can call nearly any phone in the entire world for free. Another thing that makes EvaPhone unique is how incredibly short that free call is. Free calls range from ten seconds to one minute in length, depending on the destination. You're also also limited to just two calls per day.

5. Tuitalk

Tuitalk is another Internet phone that works much like EvaPhone. It allows you to make free phone calls to around 40 countries. Each country in which you make your free phone call is limited to a certain number of minutes per call and per day. For most countries, your free Internet phone call can be six minutes in length.

Notes:

1. soft phone：软电话。
2. Google Talk browser plug-in：谷歌聊天浏览器插件。

Exercise A: Answer the following questions.

1. What are the 5 ways to make free Internet phone calls?
2. What will you have to do to make a free call using an Internet phone?
3. What is the limitation of Freebuzzer?
4. What do you know about Tuitalk?

Exercise B: Fill in the blanks.

1. With Google Voice, you can ________, free PC to phone calls, and free PC to PC calls.
2. With iCall, you can make free calls ______________ software.
3. What makes EvaPhone unique is that you can call ______________ for free.
4. Tuitalk allows you to ______________ to around 40 countries.

Step 3 Practice

I. Discuss in pairs.

1. Why do they supply free Internet phone calls?
2. Your experiences in using the Internet telephone.
3. Some day the Internet telephone will take the place of mobile phones.

II. Talk about the following pictures and guess when they were used.

Step 4 Supplementary Reading

What is Skype?

The Most Popular Voice Service

With more than 500 million registered users, Skype is the most popular voice communication service in the world. The Skype service comes with an application software, called a softphone, which is why many people think of Skype as being only a software, overlooking the great service behind.

Skype has broken many barriers to communication. While in the past you needed to take particular care of the minutes and seconds you spend speaking on international calls, you no longer need to bother about that now. If you use Skype to make PC to PC communication, you pay nothing more than the monthly Internet service, which you would anyway have paid without Skype[1].

Skype is changing how people communicate with the integration of voice and IM (Instant Messaging) into one application. Talk when you want and type when you want, and switch between the two as you wish, seamlessly[2].

High Quality

People use Skype mainly for the high quality of voice it offers and especially because it offers free PC to PC service. People around the world use Skype for several things: for long-distance meetings with family, friends and loved ones; for remote activity monitoring[3]; for business calls; for long-distance conferences; for cheap calls during travel etc.

Use it Anywhere

Skype is used in nearly all countries of the world, as it has been developed in view of delivering clear and consistent calls over the Internet. Today, there are many Skype user groups around the world. The largest groups are found in Europe, North America and South East Asia.

Notes:

1. which you would anyway have paid without Skype：没有 Skype 也要付同样多的费用。
2. switch between the two as you wish，seamlessly：在两者之间随意进行无缝转换。
3. remote activity monitoring：远程活动监视。

True or false. Correct the false statements.

1. It is not proper for many people think of Skype as being only a software.
2. While speaking on international calls，you have to bother about the minutes and seconds you spend.
3. Skype is changing how people communicate with the integration of voice and Instant Messaging into one application.
4. People use Skype mainly for the high quality of voice it offers and especially because it offers PC to PC service.
5. Skype can be used all over the world，as it has been developed in view of delivering clear and consistent calls over the Internet.

5. Telephone Functions

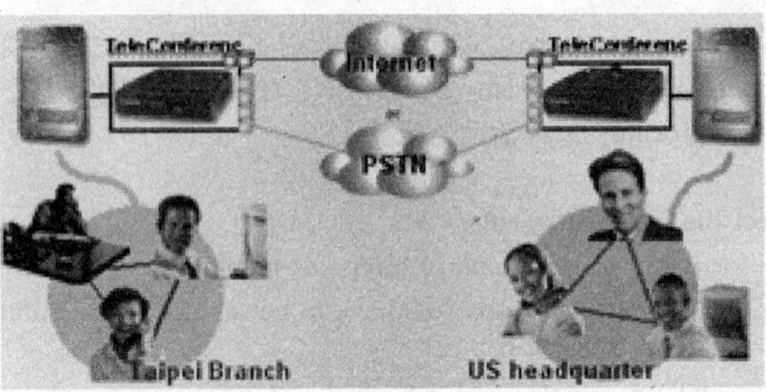

Step 1 New Words and Expressions

cater for 顾及;为……提供所需;迎合……
initiate *v.* 开始;创始;开始实施
interconnect *v.* 使互相连接,使互相联系
multiple *adj.* 由许多部分组成的,复合的;多样的
participant *n.* 关系者;参与者
transfer *v.* 转换;调动
utilize *v.* 利用,使用
voicemail *n.* 语音邮件

Step 2 Reading

A. Talk about the following topic in English.

How many telephone functions can you think of? Share your opinion with your classmates.

B. Read the passage and do the exercises.

Telephone Functions

There are a number of telephone functions that you will find useful in your workplace. These functions include transferring calls, conference calls, voicemail and answering machines[1].

Transferring Calls and Putting Calls on Hold

Sometimes before transferring a call, you may need to put the caller on hold[2]. This can happen:

- when locating the person to whom the caller wishes to speak.
- when contacting another extension to obtain information requested by the caller.
- when the caller wishes to speak to someone whose phone extension is temporarily engaged.
- when you are completing a previous call.

Conference Calls

A teleconference call may have three or more people or groups of people linked to separate phone lines. For this call, you could use a system such as Conference Master, which can cater for up to 20 participants in 20 different locations[3]. All participants can hear and contribute to the meeting.

Voicemail

Voicemail is a computer-based system that works in conjunction with your organization's PABX system[4]. Here are some of the features you will find in most voicemail systems. They can:

- send messages to an individual.
- send messages to a group.
- broadcast a message to all users.
- specify a time for a message to be sent.
- play a date and time of calls[5] at the beginning or end of a message, if required.

Answering Machines

These are useful when people are away from their desks and phones and yet they still need to be available to clients. An answering machine allows the caller to leave a message when the person is away from their phone while at work, or even after work hours.

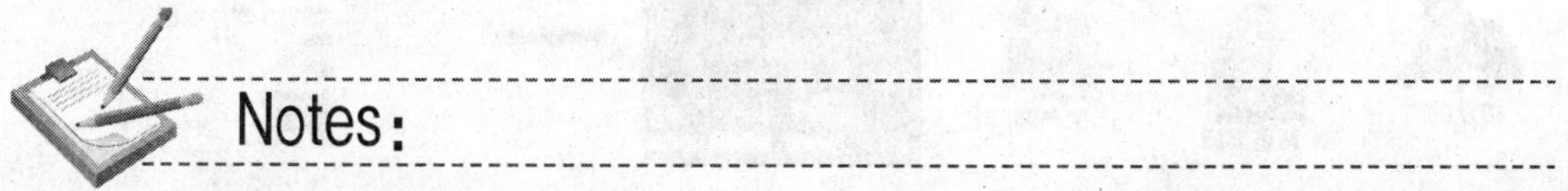

1. transferring calls, conference calls, voicemail and answering machines：转接电话，电话会议，语音邮件，答录机。
2. put the caller on hold：让对方等待。
3. cater for up to 20 participants in 20 different locations：最多可为 20 个不同地点的 20 名与会者提供服务。
4. in conjunction with your organization's PABX system：与你公司的电话通讯系统相结合。PABX：Private Automatic Branch Exchange 的缩写，即自动用户小交换机。
5. play a date and time of calls：播放来电的日期和时间。

Exercise A: Answer the following questions.

1. What telephone functions can you find useful in the workplace?

2. In what kind of situation will you need to put the caller on hold?
3. For a teleconference call, what system do you have to use?
4. What are the main features in most voicemail systems?
5. What is the main function of an answering machine?

Exercise B: Fill in the blanks.

1. Telephone functions include ______________, ______________, voicemail and answering machines.
2. You may need to ______________ when the caller wishes to speak to someone whose phone extension is temporarily engaged.
3. A teleconference call may have three or more people or groups of people ________.
4. Voicemail is a computer-based system that works ____________________ PABX system.

Step 3 Practice

I. Discuss in pairs.

1. How is a conference call in a company?
2. What will you say when you have to transfer a call?
3. Have you ever used an answering machine? If not, imagine how to use it.

II. Talk about the following pictures.

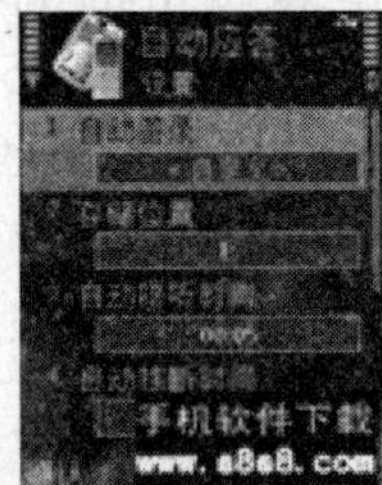

Step 4 Supplementary Reading

Conference Phones

Conference phones are used to initiate and conduct conference calls, which enable multiple callers[1] to listen and/or talk on the same call. In a conference call, the host participants[2] typically run the call with a conference phone, while remote participants dial in to a number that connects them to a conference bridge that links the various telephone lines together. Conference calls are frequently used for business meetings and corporate earnings reports, and are also commonly paired with Web conferences[3] for online presentations and sharing documents.

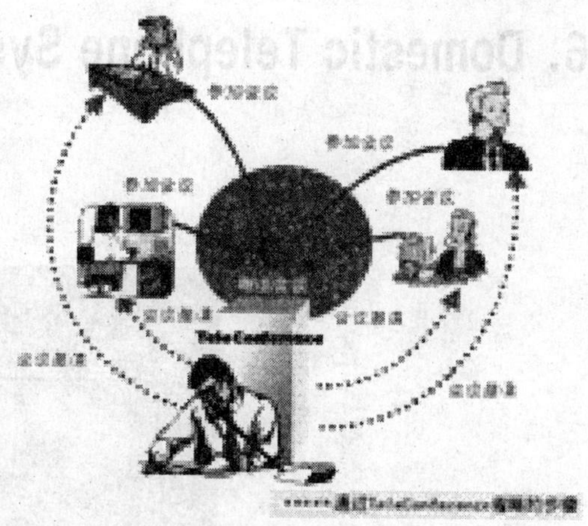

Business Telephone

A system where multiple telephones are used by businesses in an interconnected fashion[4] that allows for features such as call handling and transferring, conference calling, call metering and accounting, private and shared voice message boxes[5], etc. A business telephone system can range from just a few phones in a small business up to a complex private branch exchange (PBX) system[6] utilized by large businesses.

Business phone systems can function over the Public Switched Telephone Network (PSTN)[7] and/or over the Internet (Internet telephony or VoIP[8]). Business telephone systems can also be delivered as a hosted service (typically referred to as a centrex[9]), which can free companies from having to invest in costly equipment.

Notes:

1. multiple callers：多位打电话者。
2. host participants：主持方。
3. paired with Web conferences：与网络会议一起。
4. an interconnected fashion：以一种互联的方式。
5. call metering and accounting, private and shared voice message boxes：电话计费和结算，私人和共享的语音信息盒。
6. private branch exchange (PBX) system：用户交换机。
7. Public Switched Telephone Network (PSTN)：公共电话交换网络。
8. Internet telephony or VoIP：互联网电话或互联网协议电话。
9. centrex：中心交换机，俗称虚拟小交换机。

True or false. Correct the false statements.

1. Conference phones are used to enable multiple callers to listen and/or talk on the same call.
2. Conference calls are often used for business meetings and corporate earnings reports.
3. A business telephone system is a complex private branch exchange (PBX) system.
4. Business telephone systems can free a hosted service, which can bring down companies' cost.

6. Domestic Telephone Systems

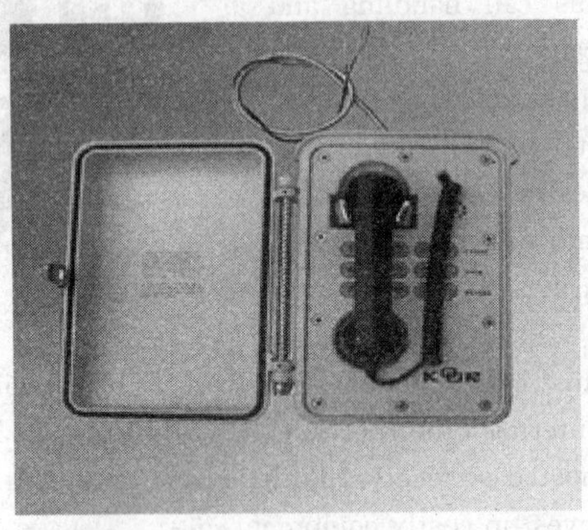

Step 1 New Words and Expressions

China Telecom 中国电信
China Unicom 中国联通
China Netcom 中国网通
China Mobile 中国移动
Ministry *n.* 部
DDD (Direct Distance Dialing) 直拨长途电话
IDD (International direct dialing) 国际直拨电话
coverage *n.* 覆盖
access *n.* 通路
v. 接通
voice quality 音质
congestion *n.* 拥堵
private data 私人数据
transmission *n.* 传输速度
account transfer 转账

Step 2 Reading

A. Talk about the following pictures in English.

B. Read the passage and do the exercises.

At present, there are four network firms — China Telecom, China Unicom, China Netcom (in 2009 China Netcom combined with China Unicom) and China Mobile[1] — that are allowed to operate IP services[2] in China. Each company has its advantages in the following four aspects of services.

1. Charge

As the Ministry of Information Industry co-ordinates, the charges of IP calls of the four companies are the same, 0.30 yuan per minute for DDD calls[3], 4.80 yuan per minute for IDD calls[4], 2.50 yuan for calls from the mainland to Hong Kong, Macao, and Taiwan, and 1.50 yuan from Shenzhen to Hong Kong, Zhongshan and Zhuhai to Macao. IP callers don't enjoy discount on holidays.

2. Range

China Telecom has the widest coverage[5]. All cities in China with telephone access and most countries in the world are open to China Telecom's IP card.

China Unicom's IP card can reach 29 cities and more than 130 countries and regions worldwide.

China Netcom's IP card can reach 14 cities in China and 149 countries and regions in the world.

China Mobile's IP card is open to only 6 cities nationwide but can access more than 200 countries and regions worldwide.

3. Voice Quality

China Telecom realizes its IP service by the public Internet, therefore net congestion and voice delay[6] may sometimes disturb conversations. The other three companies have their private data networks, which help to increase transmission speeds and improve voice quality.

4. Other Services

China Telecom and China Mobile offer account transfer services[7]. Users can transfer the remaining sum of money on one card to another card.

China Netcom links its services with bank cards. One can enjoy IP service without an IP card. Bank card users can make IP phone with their bank card numbers, so they needn't buy new IP cards and remember the new numbers again and again.

As for customer service, China Telecom, China Unicom and China Mobile provide free hotline service, while Netcom charges for its services.

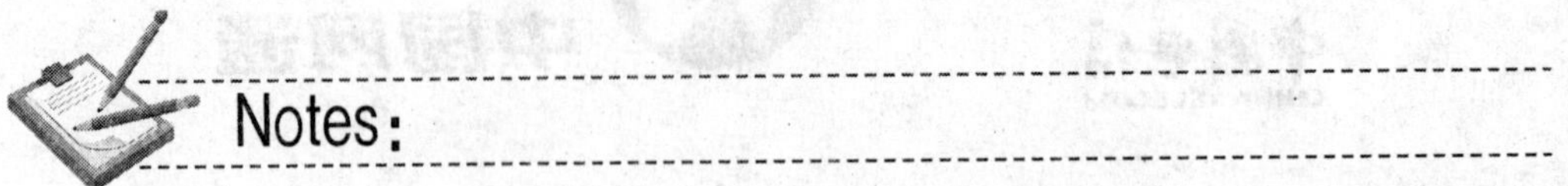

1. China Telecom, China Unicom, China Netcom (in 2009 China Netcom combined with China Unicom) and China Mobile：中国电信、中国联通、中国网通(2009 年中国网通与中国联通合并)与中国移动。
2. IP services：Internet Protocol services：网际协议服务。
3. DDD calls：直拨长途电话。
4. IDD calls：国际直拨电话。
5. has the widest coverage：拥有最广泛的覆盖范围。
6. net congestion and voice delay：网络拥塞和语音延迟。
7. account transfer services：账户转账服务。

Exercise A：Answer the following questions.

1. How many network firms are mentioned in the passage? What are they?
2. How much should Chinese IP callers pay for DDD calls?
3. Which company doesn't use the private data network in IP service?
4. What do account transfer services mean?
5. Must people buy an IP card if they want to enjoy IP service of China Netcom?

Exercise B：Fill in the blanks.

1. Each company has its advantages in the following ____________ aspects of services.
2. People should pay ____________ yuan if he makes a three-minute DDD call.
3. ____ have their private data networks.

4. ________________ charges for its customer services.

Exercise C: True or false. Correct the false statements.

1. China Unicom charges IDD calls more than the other three firms.
2. China Telecom accesses many more cities nationwide than the other three.
3. China Netcom is the only one to be allowed to operate IP service.
4. China Telecom has the widest coverage and the best voice quality.
5. Network firms seem to be more interested in providing international service.

Step 3 Practice

I. Discuss in pairs.

1. Which tools of communication do you often use?
2. What are the differences among all these tools?
3. In your opinion, which way of communication is better?

II. Talk about the following pictures and discuss their advantages and disadvantages.

Step 4 Supplementary Reading

Most British telephone cards are just plain green[1], but card collecting is becoming a popular

hobby in Britain and collectors even have their own magazine, International Telephone Cards. One reason for their interest is that cards from around the world come in a wide variety of different and often very attractive designs[2]. There are 100,000 different cards in Japan alone, and there you can put your own design onto a blank card simply by using a photograph or a business card.

The first telephone cards, produced in 1976, were Italian. Five years later the first British card appeared, and now you can buy cards in more than a hundred countries. People usually start collecting cards because they are attractive, small and light, and they do not need much space. It is also a cheap hobby for beginners, although for some people it becomes a serious business. In Paris, for example, there is a market where you can buy only telephone cards, and some French cards cost up to 4,000 pounds. The first Japanese cards have a value of about 28,000 pounds. Most people only see cards with prices like these in their collectors magazines[3].

Notes:

1. just plain green:普通的绿色。
2. come in a wide variety of different and often very attractive designs：各种不同且非常具有吸引力的设计。
3. in their collectors magazines：在他们收藏家的杂志。

Comprehension questions.

1. The text is mainly about ________.
   A. the history of phone cards
   B. phone card collecting as a hobby
   C. reason for phone card collecting
   D. the great variety of phone cards

2. When did people in Britain begin to use phone cards? ________.
   A. In 1971　　B. In 1975　　C. In 1976　　D. In 1981

3. The main reason for most people to collect phone cards is that ________.
   A. they find the cards beautiful and easy to keep
   B. they like to have something from different countries

C. they want to make money with cards
D. they think the cards are convenient to use

4. The writer mentions a market in Paris in order to show that ________.
A. card collecting is popular among young people
B. French and Japanese cards are the most valuable
C. People can make money out of card collecting
D. Card collecting magazines are very useful

7. International Telephone Systems

Step 1　New Words and Expressions

a reserve charge call　对方付费电话
additional　*a.* 附加的
direct dialing call　直拨电话
domestic　*a.* 本国的，国内的
DST　经济时(即夏令时)
GMT (Greenwich Mean Time)　格林尼治标准时间
office hours　办公时间
particular　*a.* 特定的
standard rate　标准收费率

Step 2　Reading

Read the passage and do the exercises.

You can use the Business Telecard International at any card phone in the United Kingdom. Here is some information about making international phone calls.

You can now phone almost any country in the world, although in some cases you can only call big cities. When you cannot make direct dialing calls, you can ask the international operator to help you. This is more expensive and takes more time, but it may be helpful. If you want to speak to a particular person and no one else, in this case you should ask for a "person-to-person" call. Even more expensive is a reserve charge call[1], where the person who receives the call pays.

If the international line is busy, you can reserve a call to explain the number you want and the operator will call back when the line is free. You can save money by calling outside office hours, for example, early in the morning, late at night and on Sundays. Remember that the time may be different in the country you are calling. International time is based on GMT (Greenwich Mean Time)[2]. London is on GMT and Moscow, for example, is 3 hours ahead. There is one problem: change to DST (Daylight Saving Time) for the summer. In the UK, clocks are put forward one hour in spring and put back in autumn, and so London is actually one hour ahead of GMT in the summer. You can use your Business Telecard International for domestic calls as well, but there will be an additional charge over the standard rate.

Notes:

1. reserve charge call:对方付费电话。
2. GMT (Greenwich Mean Time):格林尼治标准时间。

Exercise A: Answer the following questions.

1. What is "a reserve charge call"?
2. If you want to use your Business Telecard International, what do you have to use?
3. What is the most expensive type of call?
4. According to the passage, what can you do if the international line is busy?
5. Is it cheaper to make international phone calls at 7. a. m. than at 9. a. m. ?
6. Explain the DST for summer used in London.

Exercise B: Fill in the blanks.

1. If you want to speak to a particular person and no one else, in this case you should ask for ________________.
2. You can save money by calling outside office hours, for example, ______________________.
3. International time is based on ________________________.
4. You can use your Business Telecard International for ____________________________ as well.

Exercise C: True or false. Correct the false statements.

1. It is cheaper to make international phone calls at 4 p. m.
2. People can phone any place in the world directly.

3. If you want to spend less money, you should not ask the international operator to help you but make direct dialing calls.
4. Moscow is 3 hours ahead London during the summer.
5. By using your Business Telecard International, we need to pay more for making domestic calls.

B. Discuss in group which kind of international call you would like to make.

Step 3 Practice

Discuss in pairs and match the names of the countries or regions with its flag and calling code.

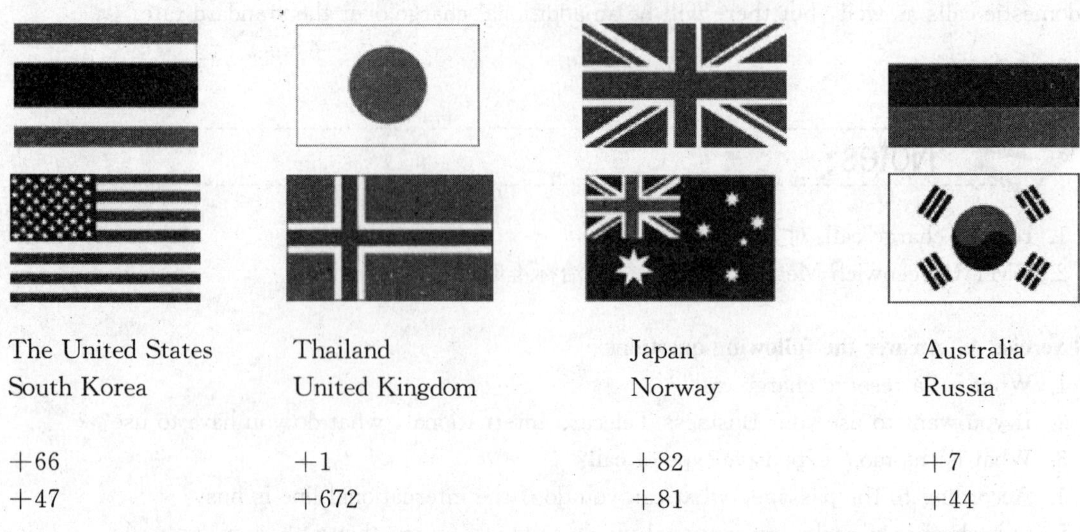

The United States	Thailand	Japan	Australia
South Korea	United Kingdom	Norway	Russia
+66	+1	+82	+7
+47	+672	+81	+44

Step 4 Supplementary Reading

Make Sure You Have the Right Cell Phone

Whether you're headed to[1] another country for business or pleasure, it is likely that you need to keep in touch with family or business partners in the United States. But if you plan to do that using your cell phone, you could have an unwelcome surprise — U. S. cell phones don't work abroad. U. S. companies use different forms of technology, not like most of the international community, including Europe.

However, there is an easy, cost-effective solution[2] to staying in touch while you're traveling. You can rent a phone that is guaranteed to work in the countries you're visiting. Roadpost[3] offers a 30-day cell phone rental plan that includes free incoming calls, free voicemail and call waiting services.

The service is convenient and simple. You can place your order online and your phone will be shipped to arrive on the date you want. If an unexpected business trip comes up, Roadpost can provide next-day delivery for most cities. In addition to the phone, Roadpost provides a spare battery, travel charger and a leather carrying case[4].

When your phone is shipped from Roadpost, you receive an e-mail confirmation that contains your international cell phone number so you can leave it with your family members and business partners; Roadpost even provides business cards preprinted with your international phone number.

Those who don't want to be without e-mail while traveling can rent an international Blackberry[5]. With an international Blackberry, you can email as much as you like, without worrying about an expensive bill. If you're traveling to very remote areas, you may want to consider renting a satellite phone. Because they receive their signals from satellites, these phones work anywhere on the planet, including oceans and mountains. When you return, simply ship the phone or Blackberry back to Roadpost using the return kit[6] the company provides.

Notes:

1. headed to:前往。
2. cost-effective solution:具有成本效益的解决方案。
3. Roadpost:美国的一家提供租用手机服务的公司。
4. a spare battery, travel charger and a leather carrying case:一个备用电池、旅行充电器和皮革手提包。
5. international Blackberry:国际性的黑莓机。
6. return kit:返回包。

Comprehension questions.

1. According to the text, Roadpost probably is ________.
   A. an organization that offers some free services
   B. a person who offers some advice to foreign tourists
   C. a company that rents cell phones to Americans going abroad
   D. a person who makes travel plans for Americans
2. The first paragraph mainly tells us that ________.
   A. Americans need to change their cell phones
   B. European form of technology is different from America's
   C. U. S. cell phones don't work abroad
   D. Americans who go abroad will meet an unwelcome surprise
3. Which of the following will help you a lot in mountainous areas?
   A. Blackberry　　B. The return kit
   C. E-mail　　D. Satellite phones
4. According to the text, it can be inferred that ________.
   A. an international Blackberry is mainly used to send e-mail
   B. Roadpost can offer cell phones using in different areas
   C. you should select a bag used to send your cell phone
   D. Roadpost's service is convenient and simple
5. Which of the free services can you get from Roadpost ________.
   A. Voicemail　　B. Sending e-mail
   C. Shipping the phone back　　D. Call waiting services

8. Basic Telephone Skills and Techniques

Step 1 New Words and Expressions

apt *a.* 倾向于
perception *n.* 观念,看法
boost *v.* 改善
exhale *n.* 呼出
function *n.* 职务
merchandise *n.* 商品,货物
multitasking *n.* 多重任务处理
smooth *a.* 顺利的

Step 2 Reading

A. Look at this list of good phone manners. Which ones would impress you?

- The call is answered promptly and you're greeted by a pleasant voice.
- The person identifies their organization and themselves.
- The person asks you your name and uses it during the conversation.
- You're correctly asked if you want to leave a message and it is taken down correctly.
- The call is ended pleasantly.

B. Read the passage and do the exercises.

When you think about your phone calls that way, you are more apt to answer the phone with a little more expectation in your voice rather than disgust[1]. If you train your employees to do the same, you will start looking at your phone as a sales building tool[2]. There are interesting statistics that show people develop a perception about you[3] within the first 30 seconds of a phone conversation and their final opinion of you in the last 30 seconds. Let's look at some phone tips that will definitely boost a positive relationship[4]!

1. Breathe

Before you pick up the phone, take a deep breath. Most of us are what they call "shallow breathers[5]". We take small breathes in and out and therefore sound tired when we answer the phone. The goal is to sound like you like your job and you are glad they called[6].

Practice taking a very big breath and answering the phone at the top of that breath. You will continue speaking on the exhale of that breath[7] and the caller will hear energy in your voice! You can also practice it when you are making a call and start your breath as the phone is ringing on the other end. You'll be surprised how you feel when you use this technique. You may try it the next time your mother-in-law calls!

2. Identify yourself

Give your full name and function and /or the name of your company. Since they have taken the time to call you, you may answer the phone this way: "Thank you for calling Merchandise Concepts, this is Anne Obarski, how can I make it a great day for you?" Hokey, maybe; memorable, maybe; friendly, you bet[8]. One tip that I seem to always repeat is that of slowing down when you answer the phone or when you call to leave a message.

3. Be Sincere

If we are honest with ourselves, we are all "problem solvers" in some way. People call us on the phone to have a problem answered. It is important to put the customer's needs ahead of ours.

4. Listen attentively

Put everything down when you answer the phone! Easier said than done[9], isn't? How many times have you been in your office answering email, talking on the phone, listening to your ipod and sipping on a Starbucks? Me too. Shame on us[10]. Customers don't like to be ignored and by multitasking, we are not focused on the customer's wants and needs.

Visualize the person even if you don't know them so that you remind yourself you are engaged in a two-way conversation. If you still have trouble listening, start taking notes on what they are saying. Use a headset, if possible, to keep your hands free. By taking notes you can verify with them as well as yourself the important points of the conversation[11] and the action items that needed attention.

5. Outcome

If the phone call has been successful, the first 30 seconds established a positive perception about you through voice, tone and focus. The last 30 seconds will be when the caller finalizes their opinion about you. You can make that a positive experience by thanking them for calling, reviewing the problem you were able to solve and then most importantly, thanking them for their continued business.

The way you speak over the telephone conveys 85 percent of your message, so by focusing on the previous 5 tips you can make it a smooth flight in your business[12] each and every time your phone rings.

Notes:

1. When you think about your phone calls that way, you are more apt to answer the phone with a little more expectation in your voice rather than disgust:当你这样考虑时,你接电话时声音里可能出现更多一点期望而不是厌恶。
2. a sales building tool:一个销售工具。
3. develop a perception about you:对你形成一种看法。
4. boost a positive relationship:推动建立一种积极的关系。
5. shallow breathers:浅呼吸者。
6. sound like you like your job and you are glad they called:听起来好像你喜欢这个工作,你很高兴他们打来电话。
7. continue speaking on the exhale of that breath:在呼气中继续说话。
8. Hokey, maybe; memorable, maybe; friendly, you bet:奇怪,可能;难忘,也许;友好,的确。
9. Easier said than done:说起来容易做起来难。
10. Shame on us:太丢脸了。
11. verify with them as well as yourself the important points of the conversation:向他们也对自己确认谈话的重点。
12. make it a smooth flight in your business:令你的事业出现顺利的飞跃。

Exercise A: Answer the following questions.

1. How many suggestions did the author give in the passage? What are they?
2. Why should we take a deep breath before picking up the phone?

3. What does "identify yourself" mean?
4. Whose needs should be put at the first place?
5. What do we have to do in the last 30 seconds?
6. How much of you message can be conveyed in the phone call?

Exercise B: Fill in the blanks.

1. The statistics show that the first and last ______________ of a phone conversation will determine people's perception about you.
2. Practice taking ______________ and answering the phone at the top of that breathe.
3. If the phone call has been successful, the first 30 seconds established a ________ perception about you through voice, and tone and focus.
4. In the passage, the author gives us the following advice about 5 aspects: ______________ ______________.

Exercise C: True or false. Correct the false statements.

1. When we answer the phone, we should try to be shallow breathers.
2. When we answer the phone, we can listen to our ipod or sip a Starbuck at the same time.
3. One tip that I seem to always repeat, is that of speeding when you answer the phone or when you call to leave a message.
4. When we answer the phone, we would rather be "problem-solvers" than "problem-makers".
5. According to the statistics, we can simply pay attention to the first and last 30 seconds of a phone conversation.

Step 3 Practice

A. Which of these phone habits annoy you when you make a business phone call?

- Being put on hold without explanation.
- Being transferred without being told what's going on.
- The person on the other end doesn't use your name but calls you "love", "dear" or "mate".
- The person doesn't identify who they are.
- The person sounds uninterested and abrupt.

B. Listen to the person answering the call in this simulation. What do you think he is doing wrong? Make a list of things that shouldn't be done when you answer a phone, and suggest improvements the person could make.

Staff member: Hello

Caller: Hello. Is this Millennium Travel?

Staff member: Yep. Can I help you?
Caller: Yes, I'd like to speak to Ron Wolfe please?

Staff member: Ron's not in today. Do you want to leave a message?
Caller: Well, if there's no one else who can help me . . . (pause) Could you tell him that Melissa Duval called. I want to change one of the flights next month and I also need to change several of the hotel bookings he made for me.

Staff member: Sorry, I've just found a pen. Could you repeat that, love?
Caller: (in slightly exasperated voice) It's Melissa Duval. I want to change one of the flights I've booked and I also need to change several of the hotel bookings Ron made for me. Can you ask him to call me back on 9876 - 54323?

Staff member: Right. Got that, darling. Bye bye then (sound of phone being hung up).

Step 4 Supplementary Reading

Telephone Techniques

Three things are important when you answer a call:

- The way you greet the person and begin the conversation.
- The tone of your voice and how it conveys friendliness and interest. 1
- The way you try to establish empathy with the caller[2] by being polite, listening carefully and giving appropriate responses.

The telephone techniques can be learned. Some of the skills involved are:

— your speaking skills and the way you use your voice.
— your listening skills.
— your skill in giving feedback.

Tips on answering the phone

Telephone operations are a very important aspect of work in the business world. A client's first impression of your travel agency is often the one that lasts[3]. Also, much of the business that comes into an organization may be via the phone.

What do you say when you answer your phone at home? Most people just say, "Hello?" Others may say something like, "Hello, Jane speaking", which is an improvement on the first response as it identifies the speaker.

Here are some tips from Beverley on answering the phone at work. They are well worth your attention.

- Answer the phone as soon as you can. More than three or four rings become a distraction and an irritation[4], both to the caller and to others in the office.
- Start by lifting the receiver with your non-writing hand to avoid changing hands if you need to write. You may need to move the phone to a different place on your desk so this is more convenient.
- Greet the customer and identify yourself and your organization.
- Put a smile in your voice and the person at the other end will recognize it! It seems difficult but try it. It will improve your own attitude and make you feel better as well.

Notes:

1. conveys friendliness and interest:传递友好与兴趣。
2. establish empathy with the caller:与对话人建立同情。
3. A client's first impression of your travel agency is often the one that lasts:你的旅行社给客户留下的第一印象通常令人记忆深刻。
4. a distraction and an irritation:令人分散注意和恼怒。

True or false. Correct the false statements.

1. When you answer a call, you should try to show your friendliness and interest.
2. Much of the business that comes into an organization may be via the meeting.
3. We should answer the phone immediately.
4. It's convenient to lift the receiver with your writing hand.
5. We can just say hello to the customer at the beginning of the phone call.